MW01624155

The Best of John Keel

The Best of John Keel

Volume 1

edited by Andrew Honigman

2008
Galde Press, Inc.
Lakeville, Minnesota, U.S.A.

Printed in the United States of America

First Edition
Second Printing, 2008

Cover design by Christopher Wells

Galde Press, Inc.
PO Box 460
Lakeville, Minnesota 55044–0460

Contents

Introduction

John A. Keel has been entertaining, amazing, and infuriating readers since the 1940s. There's nobody quite like him; he's as much an anomaly as the puzzling creatures and events that he's been reporting all those years.

Alva John Kiehle was born on March 25, 1930, in Hornell, a small town in northern New York. His father was a singer and bandleader; his mother he remembers as a "lively, pretty girl with a strong sense of humor." The marriage didn't last long, however, so he was sent to his grandparents; he joined his mother and her new husband on their farm in nearby Perry when he was ten.

The insatiable Keel curiosity kicked in early. He was, he recalls, "a reading machine," and devoured books on every possible topic: science, travel, humor, electronics. Like many boys, he was enthralled by magic and aviation; he was a fan of the comic strip *Smilin' Jack* and read everything he could find on Houdini. By the time he was twelve, he had a brush with the paranormal: an attic poltergeist that answered his knocks. By fourteen, he had invested a nickel in a typing manual from the drugstore and taught himself to type. Soon, he was renting his own office, where he wrote a column for the *Perry Herald* ("Scraping the Keel"), published the school paper (*The Jester*), and mailed off stacks of magazine submissions—all while working on the family farm. By sixteen, he had discovered the heady subculture of science fiction and was publishing his own fanzine, *The Lunarite.* He even sold a piece to the *New Yorker*—quite a feat for a small-town teen.

Obviously, Perry was no place for such ambition. School held little interest for him, and his family nagged him to stick to farming. So, in 1947, he hitchhiked to Manhattan—or, more precisely, to Greenwich Village, home base for all aspiring young artists and writers. There, he set to work, editing magazines (*Poets of America* and *Limelight*, for example); and writing comic books, radio shows, TV scripts (for pioneer station WABD), and countless articles and short stories.

To the Selective Service, however, the budding author was just another healthy specimen; in 1951, they informed Mr. Keel that he was expected at his draft board. He was assigned to Frankfurt, where he served in the Armed Forces Network. His programming ideas—remote broadcasts from Frankenstein's Castle and the Great Pyramid—earned him plenty of publicity and offers for radio work after his discharge. But he was eager to see more of the world, so he emptied his bank account and headed for Cairo.

For the next few years, he traveled throughout the Middle East, supporting himself rather precariously by writing up his adventures for men's magazines (like *Saga* and *Argosy*) back in the U.S. He spotted (possibly) a UFO in Egypt and (maybe) a yeti in Sikkim, interviewed snake charmers, visited bandits and religious cults, and filmed street magicians. He even learned a version of the Indian Rope Trick, and gave a memorably botched performance of it in New Delhi. The Indian papers hailed him as a second Robert Ripley; the American magazines touted him as a man who "cannot write unless he is climbing mountains, cutting through jungles, or meeting exciting females."

Such a footloose life couldn't last forever. The authorities in Singapore declared him an "adventurer" and unceremoniously deported him. From there, it was on to Barcelona, which was not only sunny and inexpensive, but, to his delight, still had vaudeville.

In Spain, he worked his experiences into his first book, *Jadoo* (the Indian word for "magic"). It was published in 1957; he moved back to Manhattan and promoted it by charming cobras in the window of a Times Square pet shop. And, of course, he continued writing. Funk and Wagnall's hired him as a science and geography editor; he had a syndicated newspaper column. And he re-entered television, as a writer for Goodson and Todman, where he provided material for their stable of game shows and thought up one-liners for Merv Griffin. Somewhere along the way, he even wrote two hundred episodes of a slapstick show featuring burlesque comics Mickey Deems and Joey Faye. (The show, *Mack and Meyer for Hire,* can still be found on tape; it's prized by collectors for its colorful cast of New York character actors.)

In the mid-sixties, the U.S. was hit with a UFO flap, a return of the saucer craze of the fifties. An editor at *Playboy* asked Keel for the "definitive" article. For the next few years, he tried to crack the UFO mystery, interviewing witnesses and investigating reports across the country. The phenomenon, he learned, was not a passive one. It led him into a "shadowy world," where he saw black cars vanish on country roads, pointless messages turn up in motel rooms, and his phone and mail intercepted. He concluded that UFOs, whatever they were, belonged more to the age-old stories of demons and elementals than to space travel, and summed up his findings in *Operation Trojan Horse,* still one of the essential books on the subject. In 1966, he repeatedly visited Point Pleasant, West Virginia, then the site of a particularly busy paranormal flap, with winged humanoids, disturbing Men In Black, electronic disturbances, and sheer high strangeness. The result of his investigations, *The Mothman Prophecies,* became one of his most popular books.

In the 1970s, he retreated back to the unshadowy world as a consultant for the Department of Health, Education, and Welfare, helping to streamline and cut waste in government publications. And, not so incidentally, he realized his boyhood dreams of aviation, by earning his private pilot's license. Since then, he has lived in Manhattan and Woodstock, and continued to research and report the unexplained. Among other things, he also revived the dormant New York Fortean Society, and stirred up a ufological controversy with his suggestion that the Roswell "saucer" was a Japanese Fugo balloon.

Hollywood had always been intrigued by *The Mothman Prophecies,* and Keel fielded many would-be deals over the years. In 2002, it finally came to the screen, directed by Mark Pellington. And it took, let it be noted, two actors to incarnate Keel: Richard Gere as the young reporter, and Alan Bates as the veteran theorist. The film reawakened interest in the book and led to new editions in the U.S., the UK, France, Italy, and elsewhere. The other Keelian books on the anomalous have also been through several editions, and are seldom out of print for long. Sadly, nobody has yet seen fit to reissue his classic "camp" superhero spoof from the' 60s, "The Fickle Finger of Fate," or the risqué novels that his pseudonyms have left to posterity.

Unlike many who have written on the paranormal, the occult, or the Fortean, Keel led an active—maybe even hyperactive—life, always ready to hop into a rented car and track down weirdness where and when it was happening. His wide range of interests—magic, comedy, religion, technology, philosophy, biology—gave him a broad outlook and kept him curious. And his startling ideas, hard-won by primary research and fieldwork, have kept him controversial, with equally noisy admirers and detractors.

"Beyond the Known," the column that he wrote for FATE for many years, ranged over a rich variety of topics. Sometimes he followed breaking news; sometimes he reminisced about his long stint on the paranormal beat. He had been immersed in strangeness for over thirty years by then, and knew the subject inside out. There was a new surprise to spring every month. This collection offers a lively sample of them.

He's a born storyteller, a natural wit, a provocative theorist, and—not least—a lifelong magician. Watch him closely: the Keel is quicker than the eye.

DOUG SKINNER
New York, September 2006

June 1989

Is There a Ghost in Your Computer?

Generations of science fiction writers have warned us. Hollywood has churned out scores of movies based on the premise. The day would come, they promised, when computers would develop a mind of their own; when they would start thinking without our help; when they would take over the world just as HAL took over the spaceship in *2001: A Space Odyssey* back in the 1960s.

Now it is happening!

And nobody is paying attention. The computers which we have designed and built so lovingly with transistors and microchips are now thumbing their collective circuits at us! Next year—maybe next week, even—you could be sitting in front of the boob tube watching your favorite sitcom when suddenly the picture would dissolve into an image of your late Aunt Tillie and she would soberly inform you that the jig was up. The shadowy folks in some other dimension were taking over. All of our computers and vast array of electronic gadgetry would be on their side.

Even the seemingly harmless little PCs—personal computers such as are sold in hobby shops and department stores everywhere—are joining the revolt. Eventually some smart computer will figure out that it can link up with all the other computers via telephone and form a super gigantic computer system that can independently control everything in our world from garbage pickups to nuclear missile launches. Then we'll be in a pretty pickle.

At first, stories of haunted computers seemed to belong to the Department of Untraceable Rumors (DOUR), so well-known to every Fortean investigator. Then little news stories began to appear in the back pages of newspapers. Computers were turning themselves on when nobody was around! Weird messages and indecipherable cryptographs were appearing on computer screens.

"One night there was a loud cracking noise, the power light came on and the screen lit up," Ken Hughes, editor of *Personal Computer* magazine in England reported. "Another night, random letters started flashing on the screen. I would not have believed it if I had not seen it myself. I am baffled."

Mr. Hughes had been investigating an amok computer in an office in Stockport, Cheshire. In other instances, cameras trained on computers that were not even plugged in filmed the starting switches flipping by themselves, red lights glowing, and the powerless computers flashing messages or their screens. At a convention in Virginia a few years ago, a young computer operator approached me and told me how his computer had been switching itself on and producing strange symbols on its screen. Dr. Ernst Senkowski of Mainz, West Germany, has recorded hundreds of phantom computer messages, many of which purport to be the handiwork of people who have been long dead.

Electronic Spooks

During the 1950s, when UFO-contactee mania gripped hundreds of thousands of people around the world, communication with beings from outer space became the goal of many. Amateur radio operators began to pick up mysterious signals and voices which actually told them which frequencies to tune to for a clearer signal. Sure enough, voices on those frequencies issued surprisingly convincing messages from other worlds. Communication with other planets became an established fact by 1955! Provided, of course, that you were willing to accept the rantings of "Monka" and his interplanetary cohorts as authentic. And many were. Hundreds of pamphlets and privately published books on these messages went into circulation, along with innumerable recordings. The late George Hunt Williamson, Ham operator Bob Renaud, and other electronic-oriented contactees of the period became leaders in this precarious field.

Meanwhile, a man named Attila von Szalay was trying to capture paranormal voices on the newfangled tape recorders. And he was succeeding! By running brand new tapes through his machine he was able to pick up faint voices. Others, such as Friedrich Jürgenson, a Swedish film producer, tried similar experiments and recorded voices that sometimes offered fragmentary messages, not from other planets but from the Other Side. At least the early researchers became convinced that they were receiving voices from the dead.

In the 1960s, UFO investigators were all equipped with tape recorders and Monka and his pals were abandoning shortwave radio to make clear, crisp recordings on tape. Some of these outer space tapes became big mail-order sellers. Others demonically turned UFO buffs against each other. They accused each other of hoaxing the tapes and many old friends split forever because of the ruckus. For example, in England, Norman Oliver and Eileen Buckle, two accomplished and respected investigators, had a major row over the weird voices that turned up on their tape machine while they were working on a bizarre contactee case that was later labeled "The Scorpion Mystery" by Miss Buckle, in a book with that title.

In the United States, sophisticated UFO researchers like Ivan Sanderson, Dr. Berthold Schwarz, Gray Barker, and others were all having mysterious problems with their tape recorders. It was becoming obvious that some unknown force had the ability to manipulate all of our electronic gadgets and there wasn't very much we could do about it. As if to prove the point, telephones also began to misbehave dramatically. Robotlike voices claiming to be from outer space started to call researchers all over the world. In the United States, there was an epidemic of such calls in the late 1960s. Significantly, Ma Bell did away with long-distance phone lines in that decade. Instead, the countryside was studded with microwave relay towers. Telephone calls were broadcast from tower to tower on a very narrow bead of high-frequency energy. Apparently, someone or something found these tight radio beams easy to manipulate. There was also an upsurge of phone calls from dead people to their relatives! So many, in fact, that Raymond Bayless and D. Scott Rogo compiled a book titled *Phone Calls From the Dead* in 1979.

Dr. Konstantin Raudive, a Latvian psychologist, became famous in parapsychological circles for recording some seventy-two thousand voices from the spirit world. Tape recorders began to replace Ouija boards. True, most of the voices were just whispers and mumbles, but international organizations of mumble collectors sprang up.

Haunted Television Sets

A West German named Klaus Schreiber entered the Twilight Zone in 1985 when he began to receive images of deceased persons on his television set! The dead movie star Romy Schnieder appeared on his screen, as did his late wife. Audio communications also occurred, telling him how to adjust his set and tune the frequency to get better reception. More remarkable, his experiments were repeatable. Others were able to duplicate his feat. Hans-Otto Koenig went public with this system for communicating with the dead by broadcasting over Radio Luxembourg to an audience of two million people throughout Europe. Using very sophisticated electronic apparatus enhanced by ultraviolet and infrared lights, Koenig has achieved contacts with the known dead and flabbergasted skeptical scientists.

Mr. Schreiber passed away on January 7, 1988, and he has since appeared on the television screens of experimenters following in his footsteps!

Oddly enough, none of this has received extensive publicity in the United States, although it is all very well known in Europe.

Who's Calling?

A husband-and-wife team, Jules and Maggie Harsch-Fischbach, have actually been receiving long, detailed answers, allegedly from dead people, on their computer. They also claim to be getting messages from a dead scientist on an ordinary telephone answering machine.

Have spirit forces really zeroed in on this electronic age? Or is there a new game afoot here? Are the voices claiming to be from other planets just a variation on the age-old phenomenon of the dead who have also spoken to us through trumpets, automatic writing, and spirit mediums? The talkative space people have been able to identify themselves to the full satisfaction of the UFO buffs, just as the phantom phone callers have sounded exactly like deceased people. Are all these things merely the manipulations of a force that is able to control electrical circuits and play little games with us?

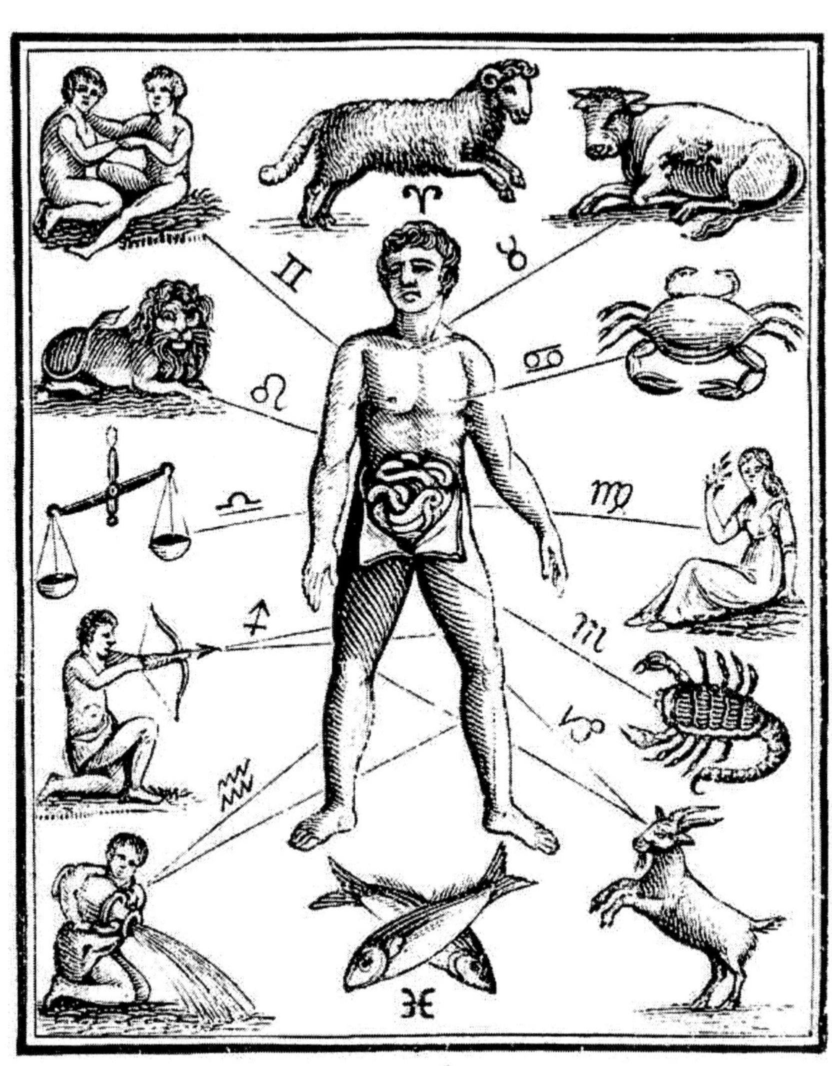

July 1989

Mysterious Influences

Don't shoot your astrologer! It's not his or her fault that your horoscope is a mess and that your whole life seems to be misaligned with the stars. Our dreary little planet is going through a bad phase. . .one that is man-made and totally out of whack with celestial movements. If we continue to muck up the cosmos, your birth sign will become as reliable as a sundial in an eclipse.

Astrologers in ancient Mesopotamia had it made. This planet, and our whole solar system, moved in reliable patterns, century after century. The actual mechanics of Earth—the magnetic field, the gravity field, the naturally electrical atmosphere—were all reasonably constant, and measurable. In addition, there were great unseen force fields in space (probable effects of the hypothetical Big Bang) that our sun and planets were sailing through at periodic intervals. Then, of course, there were minuscule waves of energy gushing across the cosmos from other stars to set up tiny reverberations in our electrical/gravitational environment. Thousands of years ago, great thinkers and brilliant mathematicians became aware of the warp and woof of the universe and countless generations studied the stars and all of these other factors, slowly developing the notion that lifeforms on this planet were often greatly affected by energy patterns from very distant sources. The science of astrology was based upon all this information.

Present-day astrologers still use fragments of that ancient knowledge, including the charts and mathematical tables that were worked out long ago by learned men on remote deserts. Until about one hundred years ago, the astrological methodology worked fairly well. People born at certain times of the year were predictably different in personality, character, and attitude from those born at other times. By studying millions of people, as well as their stars, astrologers were able to sort out and catalog these differences.

No matter how bizarre and irrational the system seemed to those of skeptical bent, it did work. Human life, and probably all other forms of life here, were unquestionably influenced by energies from out there somewhere.

Spaceship Earth

Until the 1960s, humanity was rather arrogant about its place in the universe. Then our own space program created a cultural shock. We suddenly saw our home planet as it really is—a tiny blue and white speck in the incomprehensible vastness of space. This discovery made us rather nervous and we launched a very, very expensive search for life elsewhere in the universe. We didn't find any. But our radio telescopes did pick up all manner of strange noises from energy waves that were normally invisible to us. Great stars called pulsars and quasars were pumping electrical static into space. Other great objects existed beyond the very limited range of human eyesight (our eyes can only see a small portion of the electromagnetic spectrum), pouring infrared and ultraviolet waves across trillions of miles of space. Undoubtedly, all of this energy has some effect on us, too, even though the astrologers never knew of them and so never accounted for them in their calculations.

Back on the desert in Mesopotamia, the early astrologers could study these matters unimpeded by anything other than the simple natural forces. They didn't know anything about electricity but they made some amazing guesses. And their systems worked despite their ignorance. For example, we now know that the human animal is a delicately balanced electrical organism. Modern physicians refer to chemicals and fluids in the body as electrolytes and they are taught how important electrical conductivity is to the function of our carcasses. We actually radiate electrical energy that can be detected and measured. Radio waves on certain low frequencies can make us feel lousy…or terrific. Your body is actually tuned to seven or eight Hertz (cycles per second) on the ELF (Extremely Low Frequency) band. Some people are actually so electrified that they can't wear watches.

Some years ago there was an international scandal when the Russians were caught deliberately beaming ELF waves at the U.S. Embassy in Moscow. Personnel there were suffering from mental confusion, headaches, and other illnesses directly attributable to the Soviet radio signals.

Human brains utilize electrolytes and ELF waves to act as radio transmitters and receivers. We call it ESP, and the signals can suffer interference during magnetic storms (which are common during heavy sunspot activity) and phases of the Moon. Old-fashioned "Moon Madness" is not only a reality, it is now being augmented by modern radio transmissions.

Marconi's Legacy

Until one hundred years ago, there were no man-made radio signals on this planet. Then Marconi, Tesla, and all their colleagues stumbled upon the electromagnetic spectrum and began to send electrical impulses through the air. Within a few short years there were thousands of radio stations all over the planet blanketing the world with signals on a wide range of frequencies…from the rapid pulses of UHF (ultra high frequency) television (which are only a fraction of an inch long) to the military ELF signals, which can be twenty-five hundred miles long. (Submarines and spy networks use ELF extensively.)

If your eyes were tuned to the invisible part of the spectrum you would find that you are surrounded day and night by a sea of electromagnetic radio energy. Assuming that you were sitting on Mars and looking at the Earth, you would have seen a remarkable change take place in the last one hundred years. Prior to Marconi, the Earth was a placid place marked only by a few random magnetic storms and the normal steady flow of magnetism between the poles. Since Marconi, the entire planet has been covered by a thick curtain of variegated electrical energy. Many of these signals are very harmful to plants and animals. In the 1960s, the government set up a Bureau of Radiology to study the problem of electromagnetic pollution. They found that some cities, such as Phoenix, Arizona, were bathed in so much electromagnetic pollution that many people were adversely affected...sickened. In the state if Wisconsin, where a massive Navy ELF station is in operation, local citizens have frequently protested because their phones ring endlessly with no callers on their other end, their television sets go berserk, and their hypersensitive pets cringe under furniture.

Another effect of all this electromagnetic pollution is that it has formed a huge shield over the Earth, effectively jamming many of the energies that normally flowed over us in the past—the energies that formed the basis for the beliefs of astrology, energies so weak and so subtle that their effect upon the human condition could only be calculated after thousands of years of observation and study. Now that we are living at the bottom of a well filled with electromagnetic sewage, astrology may not be a working concept anymore. A horoscope drawn up by a well-trained, dedicated astrologer today may be far less precise than the same horoscope would have been a hundred years ago. So don't shoot your astrologer if he tells you that you're going to get rich on Tuesday and you break your leg instead!

Examine your daily newspapers and you will find plenty of evidence that the human condition has changed in exact ratio to the introduction of electromagnetic pollution. The acts of madness that were once reserved for those periods when the Moon was full are now becoming daily occurrences. We have created our own negative energies to upset the delicate electrolyte systems of the human body. For thousands of years, our bodies were adjusted to the frequencies of the cosmic energies coming in from space. Now that we have surrounded ourselves with radio waves on every possible frequency, our bodies are confused and we are collectively frothing at the brain in a world where madness is becoming the norm and sanity is an anti-social condition.

August 1989

Phantom Circuses

If you wake up tomorrow morning and find a Madagascar Mooneyed Marmoset chewing on the tomato plant in your garden, and if you call in the police or the local press, you can be sure that some "expert" will quickly surface and soberly announce that the creature "obviously" escaped from a traveling circus or a private zoo. These "experts," usually professors at some local college, have been talking this kind of rubbish for generations. Every year, kangaroos, black panthers, Himalayan brown bears, giant condors, and a multitude of other peculiar non-indigenous critters march across the American landscape. And each time a cryptozoological oddity wins the attention of the press, some idiot "expert" starts mumbling about circuses and zoos.

Actually, circuses are an endangered species. Forty years ago there were over four hundred major and minor circuses traveling about the United States. Today there are fewer than forty...and only four of those travel with a real menagerie of animals.

As for private zoos, their numbers have dwindled dramatically in the past thirty years thanks to inflation and the great difficulties that have destroyed the exotic animal import business. When a creature really does escape from a zoo or circus, a very rare event, the accompanying publicity turns it into national news.

But just wait. When a vagrant kangaroo pops up in Illinois or Connecticut—and one will—the idiot experts will start babbling away about phantom circuses and private zoos.

Ghostly Toilets

On April 24, 1989, according to the Associated Press, Duane Cline was reading a newspaper in his house in Portland, Oregon, when a chunk of ice the size of a volleyball crashed through the roof into his bedroom. Mr. Cline and his wife Joan were understandably a bit miffed by this intrusion. A local "expert" immediately announced that the heavy piece of ice had "obviously" fallen from a passing airplane. While zoos and circuses have been taking the rap for our peripatetic mystery animals, airplanes have been getting the blame for the endless ice falls. Forteans know, of course, that ice has been dropping out of the sky for thousands of years, sometimes even killing livestock and, on some occasions, human beings. The "experts" always claim that the frozen lumps have come from the toilet of an airplane!

Let's talk about toilets. Oldtimers will recall that the toilets on railroad trains used to open unceremoniously onto the tracks. No flushing required. Piston-driven airliners sometimes had an arrangement whereby the contents of the toilet's tank could be discharged through a tube into the atmosphere. Sometimes this fluid could freeze and fall away from the plane in an ugly lump. In fact, some samples of ice falls analyzed in the 1960s were found to contain scented soap and human hair. So our experts concluded that all ice falls were from flying toilets. But modern jet planes do not dump their toilet tanks at thirty thousand feet. If they were rigged like trains and old prop planes, their cabins would decompress every time they tried to discharge the tank, and it is possible that passengers might even get sucked down the toilets.

Ice does form on the leading edges of the wings and other control surfaces. A mere quarter-inch of ice can be dangerous, causing a "stall" (making the wing lose lift) so ice-breaking devices are installed that shatter the ice formations into tiny pieces. Few, if any, of these pieces ever reach the ground. They melt on the way down.

Our notorious experts usually misidentify the blobs of blue ice that come crashing through our rooftops. They figure the bluishness is proof that it came from some aerial toilet. But blue ice has a name—palaeocrystic—meaning ancient ice. It is usually found in icebergs and at the South Pole. As the name implies, it is very old ice. So why—and how—is antique ice dropping on us at regular intervals?

Icebergs from Space

When the experts aren't blaming airplanes, they mumble in their beards about another explanation. And it's a doozy! They tell us that ice falls come from the tails of comets! Think about that for a moment.

Hundreds of times each day, huge chunks of metal such as solid iron, chromium, and nickel plummet into our atmosphere. We call them meteors, and the friction with the air is so intense that very few of these metallic objects ever reach the ground. They catch fire and melt on the way down. Our space capsules would have suffered the same fate if NASA had not solved the problem by coating them with a special ceramic material which melts away, absorbing the heat from the friction with the atmosphere. If solid metals melt in the plunge through our atmosphere, how can blocks of ice survive the same fall? Obviously they can't.

In order for a twenty-pound piece of ice to fall from the sky, it would have to weigh at least twenty trillion tons when it first entered our atmosphere. This would be the size of one of Jupiter's satellites!

A Russian rocket probe did find that Halley's comet, which passed through our solar system a couple of years ago, is really made of ice. Probably palaeocrystic ice at that. But if it had been on a collision course with Earth, very little of it would have survived the heat of entry.

So where is all this ice coming from? Ice falls are not a rare occurrence. Several falls are recorded each year. In addition, other forms of ice frequently drop on us. Hail storms with hailstones the size of golf balls or even bigger take place every couple of years somewhere on this planet. Some of these are composed of layers or "skins" like an onion indicating that they were formed in stages. In our upper atmosphere?

In his book, *Investigating the Unexplained,* the late Ivan T. Sanderson noted that "...there are several cases of huge slabs of ice with one surface perfectly smooth and the other festooned with icicles! Now what the hell do you make of that one?"

Thin Ice

Scientists are skating on thin ice when they try to explain these things. If outer space is really filled with gigantic icebergs, we need a sensible explanation for how they might be formed. Was there once a super planet composed of water which exploded into small fragments that immediately froze in the hostile environment of space? Are comets the remains of that planet? Are our enigmatic ice falls ancient globs of that long-forgotten world?

Back in the 1920s, Charles Fort published a book called *Lo!,* which was a study of all the strange things seen in the skies and all the odd aerial garbage that constantly rains down upon us. A renowned humorist and intellectual mischief-maker, Fort planted his tongue in his cheek and suggested that maybe there were great ice fields in the Earth's upper atmosphere. Scientists and science writers, who are not exactly known for their senses of humor, have ranted and raved about Fort's satirical remarks for generations. (They even take seriously his notion that the sky is really a piece of black velvet and the stars are merely light bulbs hanging from it.)

In the early 1960s, pilots flying rocket planes in the upper atmosphere reported back that there was "a helluva lot of ice up here." In the 1980s, a NASA ER-2 high altitude research aircraft was flown up to sixty-eight thousand feet (12.8 miles) to check the holes in the ozone layers. What did they find at that altitude? Ice...and plenty of it!

"I went into clouds at sixty-one thousand feet, and I didn't come out the whole time," pilot Ron Williams told a press conference later. The clouds were composed of thick layers of ice crystals. The temperature at that altitude was minus 130 degrees Fahrenheit. Somehow moisture was drawn to that height (above the South Pole) and then frozen. We can assume that these clouds of ice could drift to other areas where the upper atmosphere was warmer, break up, and rain down.

If ice was the only thing falling from the sky we could shrug it off with the above discovery. Unfortunately, ice is only one of many substances that keep raining on us. Blood, tons of raw meat, stone pillars, antique cannon balls, colored balls, nails, and of course fish and frogs have been showering on this planet forever. At least one of these objects has even become the centerpiece for a major religion. That's the Kaaba, the black cube that is worshiped in Mecca by all Muslims.

Let's see the aircraft toilet experts explain that.

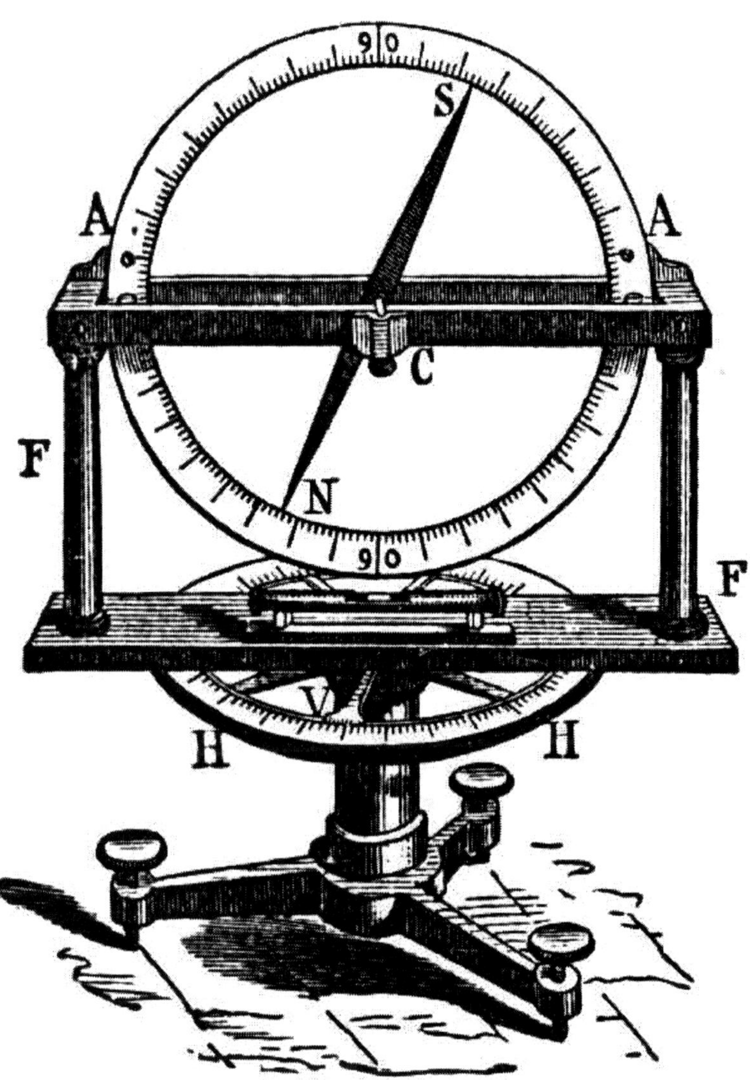
90
S
A
A
C
F
N
90
F
V
H
H

September 1989

Magic Stones

We know why the Dead Sea is dead (too salty) and the Great Bitter Lake is bitter (it tastes terrible), but nobody knows why the beautifully blue Red Sea is flecked with rusty red polkadots. These are perfect circles that remain motionless on the surface yet aren't on the surface at all. There are no mineral deposits or plants on the sea bottom reflecting the redness to the surface. The water itself contains nothing that would cause the reddish hue. Countless expeditions and divers have splashed around there trying to find the answer. All were unsuccessful.

In the southern part of the Red Sea there is a tiny uninhabited island which is as weird as the red polkadots surrounding it. It is a highly charged place, so magnetic that compasses become useless when ships near it, like a miniature Bermuda Triangle planted off the coast of the Arabian peninsula. It is composed mainly of magnetite, a black form of iron ore that is naturally magnetic and is often called lodestone. Magnetite deposits are found all over the world. Nothing mysterious about it. One of the largest lodestones ever found, weighing several tons, serves as the altar in the chapel in the United Nations building in New York. (It was donated by Sweden.) So if you ever happen to be wandering through the halls of the U.N. and your compass suddenly goes amok, now you'll know why.

Not so easily explained are the many places on this planet where compasses go awry even though there is no magnetite nearby. Some of these spots are in ocean areas where the water runs very deep. Again, the notorious Bermuda Triangle and the famed Devil's Sea off the coast of Japan are the sites of such magnetic anomalies. The condition is not a permanent one, however, but comes and goes. It seems to be related to sunspot activity. Incidentally, our orbiting space satellites have also discovered points on this planet that periodically send concentrated radio beams into space. These radio waves don't make any sense at all and the nature of their origin is a puzzle.

If you want to locate magnetic anomalies in your area, consult the maps used by pilots and navigators. Areas of magnetic deviation are always marked on them. Some years ago, the National Geological Survey Office conducted an aeromagnetic study of the entire country and prepared maps detailing the magnetic fields. They're handy for people looking for mineral deposits.

Parapsychologists have also noted that compasses go crazy in haunted houses and places where poltergeists are present. The needle just swings in a circle or, in some cases, shifts from north to point directly at the room or spot that seems to shelter a ghostly presence. Apparently some ghosts are surrounded by a magnetic field!

When flying saucers were all the rage in the 1960s, several companies manufactured UFO detectors that were actually nothing more than magnets hanging from a wire that would react to a sudden change in the magnetic field. They worked admirably well, proving that UFOs were surrounded by a powerful magnetic flow. Or perhaps their movement through the Earth's field caused a deviation. The late Ivan T. Sanderson had one of these UFO detectors in the attic of his isolated farm in New Jersey. He finally disconnected it because it had a habit of going off in the middle of the night. He couldn't figure out whether UFOs were buzzing his house or if a ghost was residing in his attic.

The Wandering Poles

For generations, scientists have been struggling to come up with a satisfactory explanation for the oddest magnetic anomaly of all. This planet is magnetized and we have no idea how or why. We are all living in a delicate but important magnetic field. Since we are electrical organisms ourselves, the presence of this field undoubtedly has an effect on us and may even be a vital part of the mysterious system that creates and sustains life. Without a magnetic field, life may be impossible.

The Earth seems to behave like a magnet. It has a north and south magnetic pole. Its magnetism is measurable and can be charted. But something is very amiss. The magnetic poles are not stationary. They move around. A lot. The entire magnetic field drifts about fifteen miles each year. Both poles swing in a large circle roughly one hundred miles in diameter and follow a circuit that repeats itself every 960 years. This movement suggests that the source of the magnetism is not fixed, but is mobile and dynamic. It couldn't be a great lump of magnetized iron. The most popular theory has been that the core of the Earth is a mass of molten metal and this is moving around a bit and somehow generates the magnetic field. But the big flaw with this notion is that heat destroys magnetism. And it is estimated that the center of the Earth may be as hot as ten thousand degrees! When we dig into the ground it gets hotter and hotter the deeper we go. The deepest we have penetrated is the Western Deep Levels diamond mine in South Africa, which goes down sixty-eight hundred feet where it is so hot that air conditioners have to be set up every few paces. Natural magnetism gets weaker as depth increases.

Another theory, currently being bandied about in scientific circles, is that the core is a miniature atomic bomb, something like the sun, and that it is putting forth all the magnetic energy. But if this were the case, certainly some of the gases and molten rock bubbling to the surface through volcanos would show some radioactivity.

Project Mohole

A group of government engineers with time on their hands in the 1960s came up with a plan to bore a hole to the center of the Earth. It began as a joke, but some bureaucrats with tapioca brains took it seriously. Washington announced Project Mohole and set up a lavish budget to accomplish it. The ensuing publicity prodded the Soviets into action. They were not about to let the United States reach the center of the Earth first, so they set up their own Mohole project. The race was on!

If either side had bothered to consult a sixteen-year-old science student they could have learned why it couldn't be done. Instead, both sides poured millions into their respective plans. The Soviets pulled out first, very embarrassed. By the time the Americans gave up, the U.S. taxpayer had shelled out over fifty million dollars for the paperwork alone! Neither side managed to construct a single piece of hardware.

The Soviets got even with us a few years later when they announced the discovery of polywater—a new form of water that, they claimed, was the biggest thing since the splitting of the atom. Our scientists managed to squander over one hundred million dollars on that one before someone figured out that polywater was just a natural byproduct of the distillation process and had no real value.

The Earthly Dynamo

If it had been possible to dig a hole straight through the center of the Earth it might have been like sticking a pin in a balloon. The planet could have blown itself up with the sudden release of the all the fiery glop down there. The loss of the third planet would have then disrupted the gravitational mechanism of the entire solar system. The other planets would fall into erratic orbits, maybe even plunging into the Sun. All because some joker in some dull government office tired of spending his days doing crossword puzzles.

As it stands, we are all riding a gigantic dynamo. After all, when you rotate a conductor in a magnetic field, electricity is generated. Bolts of lightning are created in the atmosphere. All living things are bathed in electrical energy. Lodestones are magnetized. Mysterious beams are flashed into outer space. Vast events are set into motion. And compasses turn like pinwheels in the Bermuda Triangle.

October 1989

Great Balls of Fire

Where were you on the night of November 16, 1966? If you were outdoors you were probably gaping at the sky in awe. That was the night of the great Leonid Meteor shower, when thousands of celestial objects plunged into our atmosphere, caught fire, and hurtled to Earth like spectacular fireworks. Scientists in Arizona estimated that during one twenty-minute period the meteors zipped past at the rate of 2,300 per minute. That's 130,000 bits of blazing debris per hour!

Somewhere out there in space there is apparently a gigantic mass of boulders and chunks of iron that orbit the sun in an erratic pattern that brings it into the Earth's orbit every thirty-three years or so. The next big Leonid shower will occur sometime in 1999, probably around July.

If July 1999 sounds familiar it's because Nostradamus predicted that a "great terror" would come from the skies in that month. Some translators have assumed that he was talking about an atomic war. It is more likely that he was envisioning an attack of killer meteors. Our learned astronomers estimate that a meteor only one mile in diameter could kill every living thing on this planet if it collided with Earth in just the right spot and at the right angle. There would be shock waves, tidal waves, and all kinds of geophysical upheavals. However, there's no need to worry. Nostradamus predicted that "Mars will reign for the good cause" and maybe save us. Could it be that the planet Mars will get in the way of the killer meteor and take the shock for us? We'll just have to wait until 1999 to find out.

You don't have to wait for the next Leonid shower to see meteors, however. Thousands of objects plummet into our atmosphere every day, sizzling across our skies and, fortunately, burning out completely before they hit the planet. Remnants of a few of these have been collected and studied, though. Most of them have been made of solid iron. Others are composed of various other metals, such as nickel, and some simply have been stones. Astronomers argue about how many of these things appear on an average day, but the figure is certainly in the thousands. Their total weight before hitting our atmosphere is in the many thousands of tons. Each year about 150 meteorites are recovered after striking land. The largest one, found in South Africa in 1920, weighs 132,000 pounds.

We can assume that the Earth has been bombarded by these things since the beginning of time. The craters on the Moon were probably formed by meteor strikes, too. So we have to conclude that many millions of tons of debris have been pelting us and if we could have collected all of it together it would probably form a body much larger than the Earth itself! Was there once an iron planet that blew apart? Did that explosion form the asteroid belt—a belt of some forty-five thousand miniature moons between Mars and Jupiter—and the Leonid mass tumbling in our own orbit?

The Cosmic Stakeout

In the early days of our space program NASA scientists were worried that meteors would pose a serious threat to our spacecraft. They tried to figure out ways to armor spaceships and astronauts. But they needn't have worried. There don't seem to be any meteors in space! At least, the astronauts and cosmonauts have rarely seen any big rocks floating towards the Earth. They are not a menace to space navigation. Likewise, astronomers studying the skies rarely see any meteors before they enter the atmosphere. And some scientists have spent their entire lives looking for such things.

So where are these thousands of rocks and chunks of metal coming from every day?

A minor hazard has been the presence of micrometeorites—objects the size of grains of sand zipping through space with the speed of bullets. Some of our unmanned satellites have ceased to function after being struck by these micrometeorites. Spacesuits worn by astronauts on the moon had layers of metallic shields to protect them from those tiny particles. But even the micrometeorites are relatively rare.

We know those things are there, but where are they? Why can't the astronauts see them? Why can't the astronomers see them? Why do they always drop in remote places like Greenland, Africa, and the Australian outback? So far as we know only one person in modern history has been hit by a meteor. On November 30, 1954, a nine-pound stone crashed through the roof of a house in Sylacauga, Alabama, and clobbered Mrs. E. H. Hodges. She recovered, but her roof was never quite the same.

The Biggest Iron Glob of All

The biggest meteor in history is also the most mysterious. It probably began as a huge piece of molten iron weighing millions of tons and was surrounded by a thick cloud of gases, mostly oxygen, nitrogen, and hydrogen. A very inhospitable place, as it cooled it oozed molten rock and somehow picked up a lot of electrical energy which crashed through its smoky skies in the form of lightning. Each bolt caused hydrogen and oxygen atoms to combine into molecules of water. (Remember your high school chemistry classes when you made water with electrical sparks?) For millions of years, this process produced a steady, unending rain. Eventually over seventy percent of the iron glob was covered with water. The portions that jutted up above the seas were slowly cloaked in volcanic ash and cosmic dust (an estimated thirty thousand metric tons of the latter still settle there daily). The lightning storms continued as the glob fell into an orbit around the sun. It became the third planet, a beautiful blue and white orb that would ultimately become our tiny island home in the blackness of space.

If the Earth had settled a few million miles closer to the Sun, life would have been impossible. It would have been just a trifle too hot and the actinic rays of the Sun would have been too destructive. If it had orbited a few million miles further away, it would have been too cold. Luckily for us, the planet picked just the right orbit.

If that iron glob had not had a strong electrical field, water would never have formed. Life itself requires an electrical environment. Planets without magnetic fields probably cannot produce major life forms. Our bodies, and all other living things, are tuned to respond to the energy of the Sun and the electrical impulses of the Earth and the distant stars.

For many generations, schoolchildren were taught that the Earth was originally a chunk of the Sun that had somehow been catapulted into space. But now that we understand better the atomic process, we know the Sun is an atomic bomb and consists of a relatively small amount of material undergoing the fusion process. It could not have produced the Earth and the other planets. The Earth—that giant glob of iron—had to come from somewhere else in the universe. But where? And how?

Could it be that somewhere in our galaxy there was once a gigantic planet of metal and rock rotating around a huge star? (Our own Sun is pitifully small as stars go.) Could this hypothetical planet have been populated by great giants who blithered about in human fashion and eventually blew their planet up? Could the Earth have been a small piece of that planet, melted down by the explosion, its gravity hugging some of the planet's gases to its hurtling form?

All those meteors that daily pelt the Earth and the other planets would be part of the same great cosmic explosion: hunks of a forgotten world seeking orbits of their own.

Sharing the Universe

Ancient people felt a strong kinship with the stars, the planets, and the Earth. We have somehow lost that feeling of being one with the universe. But, as some of our religions teach, we are directly connected with each other and with all living things. This planet is a part of us. It sustains us just as the Sun nourishes plant life. Our environment is a living thing. The processes that brought it into being were so complex that they seem to extend beyond mere coincidences. If that lump of smoldering iron had not been surrounded by oxygen and hydrogen, it would have cooled to become just another lifeless mass of debris in space.

This planet may be the rarest of all celestial bodies—a perfect haven for life. But we have come to infest it like fleas, destroying our host instead of accepting our place in the universe and protecting it.

Every day thousands of pieces of some lost world careen into our atmosphere to remind us of some long-lost past and show us how our world might have been. The universe is in our every cell and, as Buckminster Fuller once observed, we are all passengers on a spaceship called Earth, speeding towards some unknown destination in the cosmos.

November 1989

Signals from Space

You didn't read about it in your local newspaper, but on October 10, 1986, a new supercomputer radio telescope developed at Harvard by one Paul Horowitz picked up an intelligent signal from a distant star galaxy. The reason you didn't hear about it is because Dr. Horowitz didn't tell anybody!

Like the many thousands of overpaid scientists who have been engaged in the thirty-year search for extraterrestrial intelligences (SETI), he did not want to be identified with the boy who cried "wolf." In the highly competitive signal-hunting business there are many secrets, and the man or woman who actually intercepts a genuine radio signal from outer space will undoubtedly receive the Nobel Prize and many other honors. So they keep their findings to themselves—while they continue to flush your tax dollars down the celestial toilet.

Since Dr. Frank Drake's pioneering OZMA effort nearly thirty years ago, many billions of dollars have been spent on the search for radio waves from out there. A score of countries, including Russia, England, France, Argentina, and even tiny Israel, have built expensive radio telescopes. Hordes of scientists and technicians have spent their lives sitting in rooms filled with complicated devices, waiting for ET to call.

Needless to say, they have all lived extremely well on the fat budgets supplied by governments, major universities, philanthropists (Steven Spielberg has kicked in $150,000 to the latest SETI venture), and humble taxpayers like yourself.

What have we received for our money?

Dr. Martin Ryle, a British radio astronomer, told a press conference twenty years ago that if he did pick up a radio message from outer space he would keep it secret for years. Maybe forever.

Gerrit Vershuur, a radio astronomer who wrote *Is Anyone Out There?*, recently observed, "If you surveyed every astronomer, you'd find a majority think searching for extraterrestrials is a waste. If you surveyed biologists, who have clear-cut views about the extremely dicey nature of evolution, you'd find that all of them consider it a waste."

We're faced with a double dilemma. Most leading authorities in such matters feel that the existence of extraterrestrials is a dead issue. Even top science-fiction writers like Arthur C. Clarke have publicly confessed that they think SETI is hopeless. On the other hand, the radio astronomers offer a wide variety of optimistic theories about life out there and after thirty years of failures they still hope to get a message saying: "Send us more Jackie Gleason shows." But they won't tell us about it when it comes!

In Search of the Nobel Prize

Back in the 1960s, Russia leaped into the SETI game and Russian scientists were soon making public pronouncements that they had intercepted signals from a mighty "radio beacon" in outer space. Around the same time, the Mullard Radio Observatory at Cambridge University in England was also picking up regular beeps from somewhere out there. They soon discovered the signals were coming from huge radio stars now known as pulsars. Since then, we have discovered that space is filled with all kinds of natural radio signals on many different frequencies. We have also learned the hard way that man-made signs from Earth keep bouncing around out there and can often be misinterpreted by the radio telescopes. (On the very first day of Dr. Drake's OZMA project he received a powerful signal that eventually proved to be coming from an earthly radar installation.)

In 1977, the Ohio State University Radio Observatory received a blast from beyond that became known as the "WOW" signal. It was a sudden peak of such intensity that a technician wrote "Wow!" on the recording tape. The frequency and location of the signal in the sky were carefully noted but the signals were never repeated.

Actually, many strange signals have been picked up in the past thirty years but they do not seem to come from fixed points in the sky. They move around constantly. Some of them do appear to be the work of an intelligence even though they don't make any sense to us. A signal from the northern part of distant space can move to the southeast in a matter of hours. So it is unlikely that these are from a fixed planet or even from a moving spaceship. They are just another one of the many mysteries of the universe.

Harvard's supercomputer signal analyzer is designed so that it cannot be tricked by normal earthly radio transmissions. It monitors some 8.4 million space radio channels simultaneously and breaks down the radio spectrum into very narrow bands. If there is only one single radio station operating out there, it should be able to find it.

But even with all its sophistication, the signal on October 10, 1986, was just another false alarm.

Boondoggles and Bombshells

Today, when a technician picks up a strange signal from outer space he notes the frequency and other data carefully. Then he sits on it. He doesn't want any other scientists to detect the same signal and maybe steal his Nobel Prize. As in almost every field of human endeavor, the radio astronomers conduct feuds, vendettas, and rivalries. Modern science is a shameless bedlam of petty jealousies and nonsensical battles for credit, honors, and imaginary respectability. Some have become immensely rich from the ET boondoggle (Dr. Carl Sagan, for example). Great corporations and government agencies such as NASA have built their budgets around the premise that intelligent life exists elsewhere in the universe. Imagine the budgets and salaries they could command if they could only come up with a tiny smidgen of proof to back that premise! The U.S. Air Force could quadruple its budget if such proof were forthcoming. NASA could claim all the money in the U.S. Treasury.

So the search for extraterrestrial intelligences is pressed forward even though thirty years of massive expenditures have yielded nothing but a few anomalous radio signals. True, we have learned things about our universe that have demolished many of the astronomical theories of the pre-1960 era. But the basic premise is still a shaky one except to a small cluster of UFO-philes.

What is needed is a policy; a plan on what to do if an ET signal actually turns up. Well, breathe easy. The International Academy of Astronautics has, in fact, endorsed a formal "Declaration of Principles Concerning Activities Following the Detection of Extraterrestrial Intelligence." The Declaration was whipped up by the American Astronomical Society in Washington, NASA, and other concerned groups. The first item states that the discoverer of the ET signal "should inform his/her or its relevant national authorities. If the evidence cannot be confirmed as indicating the existence of ETI, the discoverer may disseminate the information as appropriate to the discovery of any unknown phenomenon."

What that means is that if the signal can somehow be verified, the news should be passed along to "relevant national authorities," not, God forbid, to the public. If it can't be verified then it should be tossed in the round file, which is the way scientists generally treat "the discovery of any unknown phenomenon."

The Declaration goes on for many pages defining how the news of the signal should be shared with other radio astronomers through something called The Central Bureau for Astronomical Telegrams of the International Astronomical Union. Once this learned body has decided that the signal really is from an alien radio station—and you can imagine the years of haggling, infighting, and psychotic fits of jealousy that will take place first—"the discoverer should have the privilege of making the first public announcement." By then he/she will probably be either thoroughly discredited by their colleagues or just plain dead—suicide, most likely.

NASA is stumping now for funds in its 1990 budget to start building some new SETI stations along with the space shuttle and other items. The declaration is being passed around to various scientific organization for approval and will possibly have worldwide endorsement by 1992. Scores of minor league executives have been drawing nice salaries to accomplish this. In the end, it all means that if an ET signal is received tomorrow, the public won't hear about it for many years.

December 1989

Disappearing Stars

Is there a vast scientific conspiracy to keep the truth about the stars from an unenlightened public? Think about it. You have seen all kinds of film footage and photographs taken in space by our astronauts...the stars are conspicuously missing in most of them! Where have all the stars gone? Those "billions and billions" of celestial bodies described by Dr. Carl Sagan don't seem to exist. Are NASA officials censoring the stars?

Pioneer balloonists such as Professor Auguste Piccard were nonplused when they soared to the threshold of space and watched the brilliant blue sky shift to a deep purple and then plunge to coal black. At a mere twenty miles (maybe not so "mere" when you are going straight up) the temperature plummets to far below zero and the thinning atmosphere no longer diffuses light. The sky darkens to a hostile pit of blackness and the balloonist or astronaut is confronted with the awesome loneliness of deep space. The brightest object is the nearby sun and it tends to block out the dimmer stars.

When we stand on the Earth and gaze at the night sky we are looking through a dense veil of atmospheric gases. Light coming from distant sources is softened and spread out, something like light from a projector hitting a movie screen. And many stars are too faint to penetrate the atmosphere at all. The result is that the star-laden sky is more of an optical illusion than a reality. The actual universe is far different from what we see. In a sense, we are looking at a two-dimensional universe and we are only seeing a very small part of it at any given time.

Once we go beyond that twenty-mile limit and head into outer space we are in a completely new environment. The black vault of permanent night is speckled with tiny pinpoints of light, most of which can't be seen from the Earth at all. Familiar features like the Big Dipper vanish. Suddenly there are a thousand North Stars...or none at all, because there is no north. We are surrounded on all sides and the Earth and sun become minor specks amongst millions of others. It is as if we have gone into a great swarm of fireflies moving in many directions and glowing with many different intensities.

This is the miracle and the enigma of outer space.

The detailed star maps and charts drawn so lovingly by generations of astrologers and astronomers from their Earthly bases become utterly worthless. If we were to fly farther out into space there is no way we could find our way back to earth with such maps. We would become lost in the stars.

Klaatu, Call Home

Away from the glow of our feeble little sun, we would find the universe filled with wonders that we can never see from Earth. There are huge dark blobs everywhere. Some are mountains of stone adrift in space. Others are swirling clouds of gas so big they can consume entire galaxies. One such cloud engulfs the hundreds of stars in that tiny part of the sky called the Pleiades. (Known as the Seven Sisters to all ancient cultures, only five of the stars in the Pleiades are visible to the naked eye.) Everyone is familiar with the gigantic blackness that forms the Horse's Head nebulae. Only a few stars are able to peek around it. There are many more of these black things out there, together with great glowing orbs that seem to soar about mindlessly, defying all the laws we have invented to make our universe more comfortable.

In addition, there are immeasurable amounts of energy radiating from all these things. If the Big Bang theory is correct, all these stars, lumps, and gases are sparks and debris from the catastrophic explosion of some object of unthinkable size. Since the main product of any explosion is energy, the energy in our universe far outweighs the physical matter. There are waves and pulses of energy on all frequencies and each star and galaxy is broadcasting energy of its own. We are awash in these great fields of energy. Gravity, which is still an unexplained mystery, may be one of these spatial fields. Ancient astrologers somehow figured this out, too, and suspected there was a way to measure the influences of all this energy on the human animal. Indeed, it is probable that the earth's orbit carries it through various fields of energy at various times of the year and that the these fields do affect living organisms. The position of the stars may merely serve as a crude guide of our celestial wanderings. When certain stars are in certain positions the Earth may be passing through a specific energy field.

It is easy, relatively speaking, for us to guide a space satellite like the Voyager II away from the Earth. The scientists who devised Voyager II even included instructions on how to locate our little planet in case somebody out there happened to find it drifting through the cosmos. Their system was simple enough. The finder merely has to triangulate the radio energy from a series of distant stars in much the same way that a ship at sea can triangulate its position from distant radio stations. NASA knew that a star map per se would be useless, but maybe the hypothetical extraterrestrials who find Voyager II will know enough about radio and simple mathematics to pinpoint our little island in space.

Star voyagers would not only need a sturdy system of transport, they would also need a thorough-going knowledge of radio and electronic navigation. If we ever send men into deep space we would probably have to set up a powerful radio beacon on Earth so they could find their way back. And we would have to hope that some blood-hungry insectoid race on some distant world doesn't intercept it.

Unfortunately for our own curious race the experiences of the Soviet cosmonauts and American astronauts indicate that human beings cannot really survive prolonged travel through the gravity-free reaches of interstellar space. However, it is always possible that some new discovery in quantum mechanics will find a short cut…a Star Trek-like space warp that will enable us to skitter to the stars.

Counting Stars

Earthbound astronomers are constantly counting little specks of light on photographs and cataloging the heavens. The latest official star catalog contains eighteen million entries, naming or numbering eighteen million-plus celestial bodies and pinpointing their locations. They have barely begun their task. There are probably eighteen million stars in our galaxy alone. (In case you haven't heard, we are sitting on the edge of a huge ring of stars known as the Milky Way.) Dr. Sagan is probably right when he says there are "billions and billions" of stars out there, so many that counting them is probably a futile and worthless task. It would be like counting the grains of sand on a beach.

In a few months, NASA will be launching a specially designed telescope satellite. It will give scientists an unobstructed view of the universe. Its television camera will probably send back some astonishing pictures of things that astronomers have never been able to see through our murky atmosphere. We may finally be able to peer beyond the edge and into the great void beyond. Maybe it will be like the old keyhole gag...we'll find someone out there looking back at us!

Of course, the NASA conspiracy may continue. Their photos may come up blank like the starless pictures taken by the astronauts. The truth is that when a camera is adjusted to the bright light coming from the Earth or an astronaut's spacesuit, the lens shuts down and cuts out dimmer lights like stars. Also, without an atmosphere you have to look more closely to detect the narrow, undiffused bands of light coming from each star. They're there...by the billions. They're just a little harder to see and photograph. NASA executives are too involved in conspiracies to get their budgets increased. They are not blanking out unwelcome stars. We will be counting stars for thousand of years to come. And they will be influencing us forever.

January 1990

The Day of the Nerds

In a universe filled with mysteries and miracles, the greatest wonder of all is so small that it can't be seen with the naked eye. It is remarkably simple, but no scientist can duplicate it in his modern high-tech laboratory. Yet, one day soon some nerd with unruly hair and thick-lensed glasses will win the Nobel Prize for "discovering" what we have known for thousands of years. You can yawn when the announcement is made because you read it here first.

Metaphysicians, psychic surgeons, and those strange phantom mutilators of domestic animals have all shared this secret for generations while the scientific nerds have scoffed and sneered. It will be most ironic when one of them finally hits the jackpot by recognizing something that has been there all along.

First we must give you a little background in case you have forgotten that wonderful moment in high school when you peered into a microscope at a layer of onion. You saw a tiny world of little circles linked together by some intangible substance. They were living cells—the very basis for the world around you and the stuff from which your own body is made. Every tree, every flower, every worm, and every whale is made up of billions of these little circles. In the center of each one is a black dot—the nucleus, which contains substances known as chromosomes and DNA, which program the cell in marvelous ways and determine the characteristics of the larger organism that it forms. The study of these cells is called cytology (pronounced "sigh-tall-ogy"), and the hypothetical nerd who discovers their secret will probably call himself a cytologist.

For a very long time now we have known the chemical composition of living cells. Scientists around the world have even created artificial cells in bubbling vats. Perfect duplicates of the things you saw in that piece of onion peel so long ago have been made.

There was one big difference, though. The chemicals remained inert. The scientists could not bring them to life. Evolutionists have long assumed that life began when bolts of lightning and clouds of gases engulfed puddles of chemicals. If they were right, it should be a simple matter to create a living cell—just mix the right chemicals together and give them a shot of electricity.

Scientists tried that. Nothing happened. They have tried a million other procedures. Nothing works. They know what composes a cell but they cannot bring it to life.

Some ingredient remains missing. Our technology can rip atoms apart, but we cannot put together a single, simple living cell. Could the evolutionists be wrong? Could that missing ingredient be the mysterious force the runs the whole universe like a gigantic clock?

Walls of Unreason

Powerful electron microscopes have enabled us to examine the smallest component of living cells. We have seen the walls that surround the cellular matter and confine it to that little circle. These walls are made of a fibrous material laid out in a crosshatch pattern with plenty of holes so that food can seep through to replenish the cell. Something—we aren't exactly sure what—enables these walls to stick to the walls of their neighboring cells. So when a group of cells gets together they interlock and form a kind of living Rubik's Cube. But the union is a fragile one. Any trauma can tear the cells apart, creating a wound. Broken cells take time to grow together again and mend their walls.

The skin on your delicate tummy is composed of millions of these tiny cells. When you go into the hospital with a complaining appendix, the doctor takes a very sharp scalpel and slices through those cells. No matter how sharp the instrument may be, it does massive damage as it sheers through the cells, rupturing their walls, severing them from their neighbors, causing the chemicals of many cells to ooze out. After the operation, it will take several days for the damaged cells to repair themselves and reattach themselves to the walls of the undamaged cells. We accept this healing process as natural and don't give it much thought.

Now, suppose that your nerd cytologist hits upon a method for separating cells without rupturing their walls. Suppose he finds a way to work the cells like a zipper, disconnecting them without harm and then bringing them back together so they join instantly without a long healing process. Think of the impact of such a discovery. All surgical procedures would be revolutionized overnight. You could have your appendix removed in the morning and play a few rounds of golf that very afternoon. There would be no ugly scars. Our nerd would have his face on the cover of Time. Rick Moranis would star in a movie of his life story, dull though it may be.

Actually, this process for separating cells has been in use for thousands of years! But the surgeons and cytologists have been carefully ignoring it and even resist investigating it. They just assume that it is impossible to separate cells without rupturing them.

Magical Medicine

For at least twenty-five hundred years, someone or some thing has been mutilating animals and humans very mysteriously. Five hundred years before the birth of Christ, Zoroaster, the great religious leader, was first drawn into his religious studies because of animal mutilations in Persia. There have been periodic mutilation waves (such as the one in Great Britain in 1905) ever since. In the 1960s, a great wave of mysterious mutilations began in the northeastern U.S., spreading slowly and methodically westward in the 1970s. Farmers, cattlemen, and sheep men everywhere were in a terrible uproar while veterinarians were utterly baffled. When the incisions in the poor animals were examined under a microscope, vets discovered that the cells had not been cut. They had somehow been separated. And, in a number of cases, they were partially restored! Of course, the official explainers tried to tell the angry farmers that these amazing incisions were the work of predators and buzzards.

Police entertained many absurd theories about who was committing the animal mutilations, but the culprits were never caught and no veterinarian was ever able to explain how the operations were performed.

If they had traveled to Brazil or the Philippines they would have gotten a rude shock. Psychic surgery is widely practiced in both of those countries. Hundreds of people are operated upon daily by entranced mediums who use no medical instruments. They simply run their fingernail across the patient's body and an incision opens. As in the animal mutilations, when the incisions are examined under a microscope you can see that the cells are completely intact, not cut. After the medium has extracted all kinds of glop from the wound, he seals it up with another stroke of his finger, as if he were closing a zipper, leaving no mark and no scar. If you are a skeptical observer, he will take your own hand and guide it into the open incision so you can personally feel the patient's throbbing innards!

Typically, investigators of animal mutilations scoff at psychic surgery and the believers in psychic surgery have no interest at all in the animal mutilations. It is obvious, however, that the same identical mechanism or principle is at work in both fields. The cells are being separated without harm. It is highly probable that if appropriate studies could be launched, we could determine the exact nature of that mechanism and duplicate it in our hospital operating rooms. Scientific cytologists don't believe in animal mutilations or psychic surgery, of course, and they are unwilling to risk their illusionary reputations by looking into these subjects. But if just one properly qualified scientist should dare to take that first step of looking into a microscope, he might end up with the Nobel Prize. A minute electrical charge on the proper frequency might cause the cells to part. We do know that mediums are electrically charged people and healers often radiate a lot of electricity, so it is not illogical to assume that electricity is the key element in the phenomenon.

Since the many successive New Ages of the 1800s and 1900s are bringing science closer and closer to ancient magick, we can hope modern medicine will eventually catch up with ancient knowledge and appendix scars will become a thing of the past.

February 1990

Heaven and Its Inhabitants

Mark Twain once remarked that heaven must be a ghastly place. It was filled, he pointed out, with millions of people strumming harps...although most of them had no musical talent whatsoever. All of them were also equipped with large, feathery wings but didn't really know how to fly. Imagine the noise! Imagine the chaos! All of those amateur harpists fluttering into each other!

Twain's heaven was the image whipped up by countless artists through the centuries. All that harp playing and flying about was based on human imagination and may have sounded pretty good to people of another, simpler age, just as some black slaves on old plantations thought of heaven as a place where everyone enjoyed that ultimate luxury...shoes.

Several years ago, Russian archaeologists discovered the graves of cave dwellers who had existed about thirty thousand years ago. They had been buried with their favorite possessions and tools, along with flowers. This was an indication that even the cave men and women had some kind of belief in an afterlife, and their primitive funerary practices were emulated by the ancient Egyptians tens of thousands of years later. Perhaps some cave people experienced near-death experiences (NDEs) and had come back with tales of a golden land where there were no nasty saber-toothed tigers.

For countless generations, human beings have been having NDEs when they were ill or wounded, and their stories of involuntary trips to the edge of heaven have inspired and perpetuated many religious beliefs. They floated down a long, dark tunnel towards a blazing light. There they found Uncle George and Aunt Tillie waiting for them until something suddenly snatched them back to their hospital bed on this miserable planet. Some, a minority, found themselves in that other place where fires were blazing and all the inhabitants were moaning in pain. No harp playing here. Traditionally, people who receive this unwelcome view of hell reform on the spot and become fervid do-gooders for the remainder of their earthly lives. All of our beliefs in heaven and hell are based upon these experiences.

How Big Is Valhalla?

To the ancient Greeks, the land at the end of the tunnel was Elysium, or the Elysian Fields. The Celts had legends about the Fortunate Isles, while the Jews of the Old Testament had different terms for the three basic parts: 1) the atmosphere where the clouds gather; 2) the firmament where the stars are fixed; 3) the upper heaven, where God and his angels have set up housekeeping. Hell, however, is one of the many misinterpretations of King James' translators in the English version of the old Jewish texts. They turned the word sheol into "hell" when the word actually means "the pit" or "the grave." Many generations of Bible-thumping evangelists have made a good living by threatening their followers with this misinterpretation.

Where is heaven actually located? Ancient peoples assumed it was up there among the stars where all manner of mysterious lights and objects zoomed back and forth. In the New Testament we are even told that St. John attempted to measure the place in Revelation 21, verse 16: "And the city lieth foursquare, and the length is as large as the breadth: and he measured the city with the reed, twelve thousand furlongs. The length and breadth and the height of it are equal."

A furlong is 220 yards, so 12,000 furlongs would be 2,640,000 yards or roughly 1,500 miles long in each direction. Since this is in the Bible, it is accepted by many as the last word on the exact size of heaven. Sparing you all the mathematics involved, this means that if each heavenly personage is allowed only ten cubic feet in which to live, approximately forty-nine trillion people could exist in heaven...although they would be pretty cramped. Forty-nine trillion may seem like a lot of people, but it really isn't when you consider that thousands of generations are involved from the time of the cave dwellers to the present era. At this very moment, according to the latest United Nations estimate, there are over five billion folks on this planet battling for food, air, and a few creature comforts. Twenty years from now the population will double, and one hundred years from now the Earth will probably be more crowded than heaven.

The late Robert Ripley, of *Believe It or Not* fame, once tried to figure all this out. He calculated the number of relatives you might have already ensconced in heaven. "Now, if we take 25 years as a generation," Ripley wrote, "we find there have been 78 generations since the time of Christ. And if we count only your parents, their parents, and so on backward for that length of time, we find that you will have to meet 302,231,454, 903,657,293,676,543 different relatives."

Our own planet would not be able to hold such a tremendous number. So the heavenly city of St. John would certainly never be able to accommodate them. And if they are all wearing wings and strumming harps....

The Heavenly Traffic Jam

For the sake of argument, let's suppose that all the people from the last seventy-eight generations are on this planet, or a celestial world the size of Earth. If they are allowed only two feet of space, they would not only cover every square inch of surface, but they would be stacked up to a height of 113,236 miles!

Suppose you wanted to say hello to your dear old grandfather who happened to be located some 113,000 miles up the heap. Of course, you would have to climb—there would be no other way except to scramble up this human beanstalk like little Jack. Let's assume that you can climb half as fast as the U.S. Army marches, which is about fifteen miles per day. If you climbed at the rate of eight miles a day, you would reach your old grandpa about thirty-nine years after you started, providing you didn't get yourself kicked off for stepping on somebody's ear in the ascent. Going back down would be faster, naturally, but the whole trip would probably still take you about fifty years.

Don't cancel your reservation to heaven, though. Our anthropomorphic urges have led us to view heaven as a geographical location like Chicago or Mars. Obviously, it's not. It could not be a three-dimensional place populated by the kind of bodies we are accustomed to. The visionaries who have been regaling us with their NDEs have been wrong. Aunt Tillie and Uncle George could not exist physically at the end of that tunnel. It is more likely that the NDE is a mental process generated by a brain that is slowly being deprived of blood and oxygen. It is a form of a hallucination similar to the frequently reported phenomenon of having your whole life flash before your eyes when you are in a life-threatening situation. The brain simply releases its memories in a rush, dumping everything in a few brief seconds. The tunneling sensation is well known in other types of experiences (contact with UFOs, for example) and appears to be an explainable brain reaction.

Medical science is not so sure-footed when it comes to defining the human soul, however. Humanity has always been convinced of the existence of souls and the preservation of souls after death. If the soul is a fragment of energy rather than a physical entity, there should be plenty of room for trillions of them to be stored in great energy fields in the sky. But such energy fragments might be devoid of individuality, so Uncle George's soul might exist but could never be located and separated from all the others.

Some religions teach that old souls inhabit the bodies of newborn children, suggesting that there is a constant recycling of souls. This is the basis of the belief in reincarnation and is a foundation for a number of religions. Hundreds of millions of people accept this concept. If true, it would mean that most souls never reach heaven at all. They keep getting dragged back to this little white and blue globe. Since our population is burgeoning out of control, with more people being born than ever before, the reservoir of souls must be running dry.

And heaven must be the loneliest place in the universe.

March 1990

The Fugo Balloons

> "It was not known to the general public that during the war the Japanese were attempting to use fire balloons against the West Coast of the United States."—Stephane Groueff, *Manhattan Project: The Untold Story of the Making of the Atomic Bomb* (1967).

While American schoolchildren were engaged in scrap metal drives for the war effort in the 1940s, Japanese children were put to work on a much more imaginative project. They were asked to build large paper balloons that could be filled with hydrogen and set adrift in the jet stream. Ultimately, a total of nine thousand of the Fugo balloons were built and launched. How many finally reached the U.S. will never be known, but we do know that several did manage to make the long trip. (Incidentally, many years later it was revealed that the American scrap metal drives were a phony and that the scrap metal collected was never used. The whole thing was just a scheme to give schoolchildren a sense of participation in the war.)

Wartime Japan was faced with many critical shortages. The balloons were a practical idea because they could be made of readily available brown rice paper. Artistic Japanese children decorated the paper panels with fierce dragons, snowcapped mountains, flowers, and anti-American slogans. The panels were carefully glued together and reinforced with silken strings. An indestructible mylar-like material was used for "sails" on some balloons, with spars fashioned of a lightweight pressed-rice kind of plastic. This pseudo-plastic was widely used in Japan during the war years because wood was virtually unobtainable. It was fireproof and wouldn't melt (unlike the early plastics used in the West, such as forms of bakelite).

Each balloon was equipped with a clever altimeter and system of weights. Whenever the balloon dipped below a certain altitude, the altimeter would trigger a release that would drop a weight. When all the weights were gone and the balloon still sank to a low altitude, the altimeter would finally release the payload—an incendiary bomb. The balloons were thirty-three feet in diameter. As more and more of them were launched, they became more sophisticated. Eventually some of them were attached to tracking devices and gadgets designed to attract or confuse radar. Japanese submarines spread across the Pacific and tried to check their westward journey in an effort to ascertain if the scheme was really working.

One ingenious attachment was a simple sphere made of aluminum. It was lightweight and dangled beneath the balloon until the altimeter finally released it. When a radar beam struck the sphere, the signal would ricochet in such a way that when it returned to the radar transmitter it would produce a huge image on the tracking screen. It looked as if the radar had detected an object seven hundred to one thousand feet in diameter! The Japanese subs would know they had picked up one of their balloons, but U.S. Naval ships were totally baffled by the gigantic—and impossible—returns. After the war, the U.S. Navy even released some of their reports about these huge radar "ghosts" of the Pacific. And for many years after World War II, the spheres were found in many odd places, from Australia to the Himalayan Mountains, probably dropped by Fugo balloons that had wandered way off course.

Another anti-radar technique, developed by the British early in the war, was called "chaff" by Allied pilots. The Germans and Japanese were soon using this, too. At first it consisted of chopped up tinfoil that was dumped out of planes and caused "snow" on enemy radar screens. Later, tiny strips of aluminum foil were used. These strips were cut to the wavelengths of the radar transmitters. Some were only a few centimeters long while others, called "rope," were several feet in length. Some balloons had pieces of this stuff of varying lengths dangling from their payload. When picked up by radar, they produced a scrambled image that suggested a flight of birds. Other balloons were constructed to dump batches of chaff at periodic intervals along their flight path.

Imagine how weird some of these balloons must have looked, with silvery streamers dangling from them and wide vanes spread out to act as sails and help speed them across the Pacific. Those that managed to reach the U.S. were undoubtedly seen by thousands of people, though no one would ever suspect that they came from hostile Japan five thousand miles away.

An Incredible Coincidence

America's top secret during the war years was the Manhattan Project to build the atomic bomb. One of the super-secret plutonium processing plants was located in a barren area called Hanford in the state of Washington.

"One day a mysterious power failure occurred somewhere in the current, immediately triggering the safety controls of the reactors," according to Groueff's Manhattan Project. "What had happened? Was it sabotage? Colonel Matthias' security men swarmed into the area and imposed the strictest secrecy on all information concerning the power failure. Only the top DuPont people were informed confidentially about the cause of the trouble: a Japanese balloon."

It does seem unreal, you must admit, that a flimsy paper balloon could cross the vast Pacific on an uncontrolled flight and then effectively settle on the power lines leading to one of America's most secret-and isolated-installations. But it happened. More than once!

"At least two Japanese balloons fell in the Hanford area," Groueff states, "and one of them dropped on the power line between Bonneville and Grand Coulee, thus interrupting electric current and thereby triggering the safety mechanism of the reactors."

Only the very highest officials in the government knew that America was under siege. We now know that at least one forest fire in Canada was started by a Fugo balloon and four campers in Montana were killed by one. The latter incident set off the government censors.

"The first two balloons to be seen in the United States fell in Montana and North Dakota and were reported in the Japanese press a week later," Groueff wrote. "Since only local American newspapers had mentioned the incidents, Japanese spies were obviously reading the smallest country publications. After that any mention of the balloons in American papers was censored out."

Postwar Censorship

Fugo balloons must have been a great embarrassment to American military authorities. They eluded our radar and we had no way to combat those paper balloons constructed by schoolchildren. In typical bureaucratic fashion, our leaders had to ignore their existence and the public remained ignorant of the menace, even long after the war ended.

"On January 4, 1945, the Office of Censorship asked newspaper editors and radio broadcasters to give no publicity whatsoever to balloon incidents. This voluntary censorship was adhered to from coast to coast, a remarkable self-restraint in a free-press-conscious country...." (Japan's World War II Balloon Bomb Attacks on North America, Smithsonian Institution, 1973.)

A propaganda office, the Office of War Information (OWI), had been set up in Washington during World War II. The Office of Censorship, a branch of OWI, was primarily concerned with keeping the Manhattan Project secret. Their methodology was simple enough. They would send letters to the editors of the two-thousand-plus newspapers in the country asking them to avoid certain subjects. It worked.

"In a 'strictly confidential' note to editors and broadcasters, the Office of Censorship stated: 'Cooperation from the press and radio under this request has been excellent despite the fact that Japanese fire balloons are reaching the United States, Canada, and Mexico in increasing numbers.... There is no question that your refusal to broadcast information about these balloons has baffled the Japanese, annoyed and hindered them, and has been an important contribution to security." (Article, "Jap Balloons Dropped Bombs on U.S. During World War II" by R. C. Mikesh, *National Enquirer,* July 28, 1968.)

So we know the balloons were accidentally bombing Mexico and Canada, too. Thanks to the self-imposed censorship, we will never know just how many of the balloons reached this continent or what the total damage really was.

Still More Secrecy

Japan, somewhat unnerved by our atomic bombs, surrendered in August 1945. The war ended, our boys came home, the Office of Censorship was disbanded, and the launching of Fugo balloons ceased. But something strange happened. Fugo balloons continued to appear over the United States for years!

Every Fortean has heard the strange reports of old newspapers suddenly fluttering out of a clear sky, giving no clue as to where they had been in the months or years since they were published. Lightweight items may float around in the atmosphere for one hundred years before dropping into your backyard.

Of the nine thousand balloons sent aloft by the Japanese, it is safe to assume that most of them finally landed harmlessly in the ocean. A few reached North America, and the rest got caught in the peculiar winds and eddies of the upper stratosphere where all those old newspapers, hats, frogs, and blocks of ice drift about. Then, from time to time, one would crash to earth and thoroughly mystify all those who had never heard about the secret balloon invasion.

Almost a year after the war, one turned up on the border of Colorado and New Mexico, according to the Durango Chapbook, July 1946. "On April

19,1946, two men excitedly reported that Navajo Lake had been bombed by a flying brown thing. They said a silvery object had been dropped from a brown sphere. Just before it reached the water it exploded and showered flames in all directions. The sphere soared away."

The jet stream seemed to carry many of the balloons on a curved course from Oregon to New Mexico. In early 1947, they were still drifting down. Reports were scanty, but elements of the U.S. Army were clearly interested.

"Two big, brown paper balloons, one of which had Christmas tree 'icicles' hanging from it, were found by campers near Malheur Lake this Spring," a brief item in The West Oregonian revealed on September 27, 1947. "The remnants of a third, with a strange metal instrument attached, were found in Klamath County in August. Army personnel visited the site and removed all the debris. All three balloons appeared to be handmade, according to witnesses, and contained mysterious Oriental-like inscriptions."

A curtain of secrecy continued to shield the unwary public from the explosive balloons in their midst. The biggest breech of this security occurred in July 1947, at the height of the first flying saucer scare when, after a severe storm, the remains of one of the balloons was found on a ranch in Lincoln County, New Mexico. Local newspapers described the find, and the wire services picked up the story. Later, military authorities carted away the materials and announced it was nothing but a weather balloon. Obviously, they were determined to keep the existence of the Fugo balloons a secret two years after the war. In fact, few knew about the Fugo project until the 1950s, when a small Japanese booklet on the subject was published.

There is evidence that the balloons were still bombing New Mexico in 1949, four years after the end of hostilities. In his 1953 book, *Flying Saucers from Outer Space,* Donald Keyhoe describes the "Red Spray saucers" which appeared near Albuquerque, dropped to about two hundred feet, exploded, and sprayed fire in all directions.

There was a mysterious explosion of an incendiary-type device over a Brazilian beach in 1957. It scattered pieces of magnesium, a prime ingredient for World War II incendiary bombs, and is still considered a "crashed saucer" by UFO cultists. It does seem unlikely that a bomb launched in 1945 would turn up in Brazil twelve years later, but it is possible.

Roswell Revisited

Military secrecy worked so well that the Fugo project would have been completely forgotten if a couple of the damnable things had not knocked out the lights at Hanford and thus found immortality in the literature on the development of the atomic bomb. When the U.S. Government Printing Office published the Smithsonian's report on the subject in 1973, only a few random aviation historians paid any attention to it.

A 1950 bestseller, *Behind the Flying Saucers* by *Variety* columnist Frank Scully, embellished the New Mexico incidents with complicated tales of dead "little men," the autopsies of same, and other fanciful rumors. Although thoroughly disproven later, Scully's stories became an integral part of the burgeoning flying saucer lore known as the "Roswell Incident."

Horror novelist Whitley Strieber visited Roswell in the 1980s and tracked down some of the surviving witnesses. In the Afterword to *Majestic*, he repeats the testimony of some of the witnesses:

"Marcel went on to describe what he had found. 'There was all kinds of stuff—small beams about three-eighths or a half-inch square with some sort of hieroglyphics on them that nobody could decipher. These looked something like balsa wood, and were of about the same weight, except they were not wood at all. They were very hard, although flexible, and would not burn. There was a great deal of unusual parchment-like substance which was brown in color and extremely strong, and a great number of small pieces of a metal like tinfoil, except that it wasn't tinfoil.' Later 'Mac' Brazel's daughter Bessie described the paper as having apparent flowers pressed in it."

Unfortunately, Strieber did not have the last word. Several books and countless magazine articles have been inspired by the "Roswell Incident," and several more are due to appear in 1990 and '91. The Fugo balloons will be with us for a long time.

April 1990

Dumb Animals and Smart Plants

If you were a recent arrival from some distant star, visiting the planet Earth for the first time, you would probably want to make contact with an intelligent life form. Where would you look? Intelligence is rare in this universe, and it is especially rare on this planet. The really smart creatures are in hiding. That's why we have never caught an abominable snowman, a Bigfoot, or a Loch Ness sea serpent.

Zoological experts generally agree that there are three major creatures of high intelligence here, and thousands of minor ones. The lowly pig, for example, is very smart, as are common dogs and cats. But, since this planet is mostly water, an extraterrestrial visitor would probably look in our oceans first, and he would not be disappointed. Dr. John Lilly, Boris Said, and other scientists who have worked extensively with dolphins agree that those fascinating creatures appear to be more intelligent than human beings. Next in line are whales, followed by the majestic elephant. Primates—monkeys, gorillas, apes, and man—are rather low on the scale. There are birds and even insects that are smarter than some two-legged creatures.

When it comes to sheer dumbness, you probably know several human beings who can be outsmarted by a pig. A hill of lowly ants can display far more intelligence than a bevy of bathing beauties.

So it would be logical for a visitor from another universe to dip into our waters and pay social calls on the dolphins and other mammals of the briny deep...while ignoring all the primates who live in total chaos on the land surfaces.

The Culinary Art of Cannibalism

Most animals kill for two reasons: food or self-defense. Only two of Earth's critters kill for sport. One is the panther—a big cat. The other is that two-legged misfit called Man.

Until as recently as the 1950s, cannibalism was a very common practice among human animals on this planet. In the Pacific Islands, roasted humans were known as "long pigs." In certain tribes in Africa, you were expected to donate one of your relatives to be a main participant during feasts and festivals. The choicest part of a cooked human was said to be the palms of the hands. In South America, we not only turned our enemies into stew meat, we also plunged the skins of their heads into boiling water repeatedly until it shrank. Shrunken human heads were prize possessions in Ecuador.

You'll never catch a dolphin dining on another dolphin. Although it is true that some insects and animals indulge in cannibalism, it is frowned upon by most higher species. Many would prefer to starve. Humans, even in recent years, have been known to eat their friends and colleagues after plane crashes, shipwrecks, and natural disasters. Whales don't eat other whales, and elephants are strict vegetarians.

In India, the natives speak respectfully of "the elephant people." They recognize the fact that elephants have a social structure and very civilized patterns of behavior. They also have a sense of humor and love to play jokes on each other. When left alone, the ponderous pachyderms are quite harmless and, like the dolphins, have performed legendary feats to help humans in distress. We have repaid them by slaughtering them for their elongated teeth—their tusks—to make billiard balls and piano keys.

In the animal kingdom, natural enemies abound. Birds feed on insects. Insects feed on smaller insects. Fish gobble up smaller fish. But the dolphins, whales, and elephants have only one natural enemy. Man, alas, is the enemy of all living things. It is estimated that one hundred thousand dolphins die every year after being trapped in the nets of tuna fishermen. The great whales are well on their way to total extinction because of man's greed.

We kill them for their fatty oils and a substance called ambergris which we use to make perfume. In Africa, wild giraffes are almost extinct because we gun down these graceful animals for their tails which are turned into fly whisks to be sold to tourists! The great African elephant herds are vanishing because poachers are attacking them with military weapons. In a few more years, there will be no elephants at all. A fierce war is being waged right now between game wardens and poachers. With orders to shoot poachers on sight, the game wardens are losing the battle. More game wardens are getting killed than poachers. Elephants are dying at the rate of one hundred per day in some areas. In an effort to stem the slaughter, many countries now forbid the importation of elephant ivory.

If you have followed the ecological news, you know that other heroic humans are beating baby seals to death with baseball bats for their fur, and that the mighty rhino is on the way out because rhino horns are ground up for use as an aphrodisiac in the Orient.

A Hole in the Sky

A few hundred years ago, Manhattan Island was a peaceful body of land covered with forest and brooks inhabited by all kinds of wildlife. Today the island is a slab of concrete spewing poisonous gases into the air and occupied by millions of humans who murder and rape each other in appalling numbers. The Central Park Zoo had to be closed for a few years because the animals were dying from the gasoline fumes.

The story is the same in every corner of our little planet. Mass destruction is taking place everywhere. The waters have been polluted. The air in many places, such as Mexico City, is almost unbreathable. In Tokyo, department stores sell cans of oxygen that you can whiff as you stroll the teeming streets. Rainforests are being hacked down in South America, thus changing the weather patterns everywhere. In the next century we will run out of water, air, and food. Meanwhile, our population is out of control and will be doubling every few years. The day is not far off when a young couple will have to purchase a very expensive license giving them permission to have a child. Already, in China, couples are punished by steep taxes if they have more than one child.

A visitor from another world might take note of all this and report that the Earth is not inhabited. It is infested. We are swarming over the planet like fleas on a dog. As author Kurt Vonnegut observed, things are getting steadily worse, and nothing is ever going to get better again.

Back in the 1960s, a trio of children in Garabandal, Spain, claimed to have visions of the Virgin. They said they were told that we would know the end was near when a hole appeared in the sky. That prediction didn't make any sense to them. But now we know we have poisoned the atmosphere, and two holes have appeared in the ozone layer of the North and South Poles. Deadly cosmic rays are seeping through, adding to all the other miseries we have foisted upon ourselves. The sun's rays are already getting more intense, and cases of skin cancer are on the increase.

Once all these cataclysmic forces are unleashed, it is very difficult, if not impossible, to reverse the processes. Scientists recently estimated that the melting of the polar ice caps will cause the world's oceans to rise at least six feet by the middle of the next century. This means that many beaches will vanish forever and coastal cities will be washed away.

How to Save the World

No matter how you slice it, the Earth seems to be a doomed planet. Man, the natural enemy of all living things, has been systematically destroying it. Thousands of animals and insects are now totally extinct, thanks to us. Vast areas of once arable land are now dust bowls and deserts. Watersheds and rainforests are rapidly being depleted. We have sucked all of the planet's natural resources dry.

Earth is the only planet with life in this part of the universe. Perhaps it is the only one in a billion galaxies. It is too precious to be wasted by an infestation of cruel, stupid, cannibalistic carnivores.

There is only one solution—

The human race must go.

Six hundred years ago, the humble flea killed off over half of the human population by spreading the Black Plague. Now a new plague—AIDS—is upon us. Every continent is affected. In the Soviet Union, the official explanation is that the disease was developed by the CIA. British ufologist Gordon Creighton has speculated that the flying saucers have deliberately introduced it to this planet, implying that visitors from somewhere else have interviewed the dolphins and sized up man's catastrophic interference with nature. For a while it appeared that we would use the atomic bomb to wipe our race out, but the Cold War is melting and we are still overbreeding as we hack away at the planet.

Earthquakes, hurricanes, volcanic eruptions, the greenhouse effect, and other calamities seem to be on the increase. We have turned our beautiful little world into a garbage dump. Maybe it is fighting back. Or maybe the dolphins have struck a deal with visitors from afar, asking them to help rid the planet of all those pesky hairy bipeds before it is too late—before all the elephants, whales, giraffes, and other respectable, civilized life forms are devoured.

May 1990

Into the Void

You are walking to the corner grocery store on a beautiful spring evening. The sky is clear and the weather is perfect. Suddenly a strange fog begins to form ahead of you. It just doesn't look right. It seems almost alive as it moves toward you. It swirls around you and you feel a faint tingling sensation. The fog thickens and blinds you. You can no longer see the familiar surroundings. For a moment you stand completely enshrouded, overcome with fear and nearly suffocating in the dense mist.

Then, just as suddenly, the fog begins to dissipate. You are able to see again. But something is wrong.

Something is very wrong indeed!

Everything has changed. You are no lnger standing on a familiar street. You are in a clearing in something that looks like a jungle. Strange bird calls and animal sounds vibrate through the trees. Your mind is unclear and your memory seems garbled. You don't know who you are or where you are. Later you will discover that you are two thousand miles from home. You have somehow traversed time and space. In a split second you have gone part way around the world and it may take you many months, even years, to find your way back.

Such nightmares are not science fiction fantasies. They happen several times a year to ordinary people like yourself. A man is mowing the lawn in his backyard. His wife hears the mower suddenly stop. She looks outside and sees that the mower is there but her husband isn't. She will never see him again.

A waitress leaves a restaurant to put a coin in a parking meter. She never comes back.

A small, single-engine plane flies into a tiny cloud above an airport and, in front of many witnesses, never reappears.

One celebrated report of this type tells how eight hundred soldiers in World War I marched into a low-hanging cloud on a battlefield. They all vanished forever!

Where is Everybody Going?

Human beings, animals, and all kinds of objects have been traveling through time and space involuntarily since the beginning of time. The extensive records of religion, occultism, and psychic phenomena are filled with such accounts. You don't have to visit the Bermuda Triangle in the Atlantic or the notorious Devil's Sea off the coast of Japan to be caught up in one of these "vile vortices," as the late Ivan Sanderson dubbed them.

Drivers have reported seeing other cars vanish on busy highways. Other drivers have claimed that they traveled impossible distances in a very short time. UFO lore is loaded with tales of people and automobiles finding some shortcut in our three-dimensional world. As Charles Fort pointed out in the 1920s, teleportation is an actual fact of nature.

It is not a rare occurrence.

It happens all the time.

There was once a private museum in California that displayed nothing but objects that had supposedly been teleported.

The key issue stemming from these events is simple enough: What makes these things happen?

Hot Rocks from Cold Skies

Every year somewhere on this planet stones begin to drop from the sky. They usually pelt some random house, pounding down on the roof continuously for several days. Local police and newspaper reporters invariably gather to witness this curiosity and create ridiculous theories to explain it. The people who live in the troubled house often move away.

The stones, usually pebbles and small rocks, come out of a clear sky, often seeming to move in slow motion. They are frequently warm, even hot to the touch. Police officials try to blame "teenagers," and they search the area for mischievous youngsters who, they think, are hiding in the bushes, heating stones over some kind of fire, and shooting them at the house with slingshots. Instead of tiring quickly of the game, as teenagers are wont to do, the police theorize that the kids keep up the silly barrage all day and all night for several days—in some cases, several weeks.

Collectors of Forteana know that cases of these rainstorms of rocks have taken place on every continent. This year it could happen in a village in Africa or a town in South America. There are even documented cases in which the stones have chosen to pound away at tents on the Sahara Desert. The police reaction is always the same—it must be those damned teenagers.

I once visited a house in Calcutta, India, where the stones were dropping from the ceiling inside the house. The owner had to take a shovel and shovel out his living room every morning! The stones seemed to materialize suddenly an inch or two below the ceiling and then drop slowly. If you placed a plate under the dropping stone, the rock would somehow curve and miss the plate. Some parapsychologists view this as a form of poltergeist phenomena and it is often discussed in books about poltergeists.

We don't know where the disappearing people go, and we certainly don't know where the appearing rocks come from. Is there a gravel pit in some hypothetical alternate dimension where all the gravel is slowly filtering through some aberrant black hole and raining down on us?

It's Not Like *The Fly*

There are very few clues in these teleportation cases that might lead us to a solution. We do know that teleported objects are transferred instantly, probably outside our own time frame. Science fiction stories like *The Fly* try to explain teleportation as a kind of radio process. They speculate that the person or object is broken down atomically into energy. This energy is then radioed to a distant point where it is reconstructed into physical matter.

But the innumerable cases that occur in nature every year make such theories unlikely. The whole object or being is transferred instantly. There seems to be a warp of time and space involved.

It may be connected with the Earth's magnetic field. The mysterious fog that accompanies so many of these manifestations is clearly a byproduct of the force or forces involved. The fog may indicate that there is a sudden drop of temperature in the area of the teleportation. This temperature drop may be the natural effect of a mass of magnetic or electrical energy that is creating a "hole" in our reality or dimension. The warming of the stones is a reversal of this effect.

Another clue is the fact that teleportation incidents seem to increase during periods of high sunspot activity. We know that sunspots interfere with the Earth's magnetic field and stimulate unusual events such as UFO sightings, so it is possible that teleportation is a part of the same matrix.

When you realize how widespread the teleportation phenomenon is, it is remarkable that so few people are really involved in investigating it. Certainly the number of people chasing sea serpents and other intangibles far outweighs the handful who are studying teleportation.

We should all take greater interest. After all, you never know when a mysterious fog might gather on your front lawn and you will feel a strange, tingling sensation....

June 1990

Who's Silly Now?

It happens every June. Just as the spring thaw is finally reaching Scandinavia and the far north, someone plodding through the slush around one of the fjords of Sweden or Norway suddenly sees a fountain of bubbles and watches in amazement as a huge gray submarine roars to the surface of the icy waters. The alarm goes out. The phantom submarines are back!

For generations, dating all the way back to the early 1920s, mysterious submarines have been appearing annually in the remote and inhospitable waterways of northern Scandinavia, where few ships of any kind ever venture. And for generations the navies of several countries have tried in vain to trap them.

In the 1930s, the authorities grumbled that the subs might belong to "liquor smugglers." The Nazis got the blame in the 1940s. There were even rumors that the Germans were building elaborate underwater bases in the fjords of Norway during World War II.

In the 1960s and '70s, the Soviets were accused of sending their subs into the fjords for no apparent purpose. In 1972, the Norwegian government was nearly toppled by a major scandal when their navy had one of the subs cornered and it got away. Depth charges and the usual anti-submarine tactics fail in these cases. All sonar, radar, radio, and other electrical equipment failed simultaneously on all the Norwegian naval vessels in the '72 incident, enabling the sub—or whatever it was—to escape.

A few years ago, a Soviet submarine actually ran aground on Swedish turf and the angry Swedish government broke all diplomatic ties with the Soviet Union. But the episode did not end the mystery. The phantom subs still appear every June, just as they have been doing for seventy years, not only in Scandinavia but also in South America, Australia, and a hundred other places. Forteans even have a name for them: USOs (unidentified submarine objects).

The Silly Season

In the days when newspapers were everyone's main source of information, hard-boiled journalists referred to the summer months as "the silly season." It was a time for bathing-beauty contests, reports of phantom subs, sea serpents, and human interest stories that were ignored in the busier news periods. Today the silly season still generates silliness in the form of statements by politicians, dithering bureaucrats, and almost mindless campaigns whipped up by TV news departments trying to stimulate higher ratings with endless stories about menacing diseases, sexual weirdness, and garbage-strewn beaches. Sewer journalism has replaced the "yellow" journalism of old. Crackpotism has become the national pastime and the silly season lasts all year long.

Solstice Strangeness

Late in June, the sun does the flip-flop that we know as the summer solstice. It pauses briefly in its wanderings across the sky around June 21–24, and more strange things begin to happen. Even in very ancient times, people recognized the solstice as a very special time. The earliest religions made it an important festival day. Elaborate monuments and structures were built in such a way that the rising sun would peep through carefully designed apertures only on the day of the solstice. Even today millions of people observe the solstice with so-called "pagan" rituals and feasts.

June 24 also marks the birth of ufology. On June 24, 1947, Kenneth Arnold saw a group of strange objects whizzing around the mountains of Washington state and his report kicked off the first big flying saucer craze. The summer solstice has frequently produced a wave of saucer sightings ever since. Some think those saucers are somehow whipped up by all of those praying pagans.

Missing Minds

Every June the phantom submarines come out of hiding and while our navies are chasing USOs, the UFOs pop in for a visit. Then, as the thermometer rises, people begin to see large dark forms swimming about Loch Ness, Lake Champlain, Chesapeake Bay, and several other freshwater lakes in China, Siberia, Canada, et cetera. The monster sighting season is in full swing! The politicians polish their tongues and the silly season is well underway.

Amnesia in July

In July, another annual epidemic begins. This one is even more bizarre than all those USOs and UFOs, but it takes place very quietly and not even the FBI tries to catalog it. In police stations and hospitals all over the country, confused citizens appear and ask for help. They cannot remember who they are or where they are from. They are victims of amnesia. Some of them eventually regain their identity and return to their homes. Others are not so lucky and have to construct a whole new life for themselves. They seem to come from all walks of life, span all age groups, and are relatively normal except for the fact that their pasts have somehow been obliterated. Some prove to have come from places very far—thousands of miles away—from where they suddenly find themselves. They may have been missing from their homes for months—sometimes even for years—before they finally surfaced.

Back in the 1920s, author Charles Fort noted a few cases of this phenomenon, just as he observed that people with certain specific names seemed to be disappearing. "Someone is collecting Ambroses," he suggested. Actually, during these annual amnesia waves there do seem to be odd correlations in the names. One year the name Maddox turned up in several cases.

In another year (1969), Hill was the name of several scattered amnesia victims.

Of course, some of these incidents prove to have a very logical explanation. The victim banged his or her head, lost his memory, and wandered off. There was nothing too unusual or supernatural about it. But other cases defy logical explanations.

And why do so many of these amnesia victims surface in the month of July? That's the real puzzle. Is somebody out there still collecting Ambroses—and Hills and Maddoxes?

Phantom Vandals

Another summertime mystery that attracts very little notice is the cemetery vandalism that baffles local police everywhere. Large, heavy tombstones are found knocked over in neat rows. Many are reinforced with thick steel rods, which have been broken off like toothpicks. It would take heavy machinery like tractors to do this kind of damage. The police usually try to blame the usual imaginary bands of restless teenagers despite the dearth of footprints, tire tracks, or other tangible evidence. In case after case, as many as one hundred tombstones have been flattened in a single night. The local police never realize that the same thing has happened in scores of other cemeteries around the country. No teenager has ever been caught attacking tombstones. Real vandalism, which happens only rarely, usually consists of writing obscenities or racial remarks on the headstones in ethnic cemeteries.

These are just some of the many unusual events that go largely unnoticed every summer. It is possible, even probable, that your local newspaper will be mentioning some of them in the weeks ahead.

By the end of August, things should quiet down. Then watch out for September. About eight hundred people are killed every year by lightning and, for some peculiar reason, many of these deaths occur in the month of September. It often happens in open fields like golf courses, tennis courts, and baseball diamonds. Those who aren't killed outright when they get zapped lose their memories.

July 1990

Now it Can Be Told

A couple of hours from where you now live there is a wonderful underground city with bowling alleys, a beauty shop, a fully equipped hospital, a movie theater, and hundreds of cases of fine whiskey. If you live in a major city, it may be even closer. The one in New Orleans is right in the city itself.

These underground metropolises—there are over ninety of them—are one of the worst-kept secrets of the Cold War.

But they haven't been overpublicized, either. They sound like one of the fantasies of the late Richard Shaver (remember the "Shaver Mystery" about the underground world?) and they frequently provide fodder for the wild rumors of a whole delusionary subculture that has sprung up around them.

Old-timers will recall that back in the 1950s, when Cold War paranoia peaked, everyone started building atom bomb shelters in their backyards. We had almost no Civil Defense program, and if a nuclear war had broken out we would have been in big trouble.

In contrast, the Soviets were building shelters of heavy concrete in the basements of every new building they were erecting. The theory—part of the madness of those times—was that the nation with the most survivors would be the winner of the war!

In 1962, there was the Cuban Missile Crisis. This was a major confrontation between the U.S. and the Soviet Union. We came very close to World War III—so close that President Kennedy and Congress had to face the grim fact that our civilian population had no protection whatsoever. If war had come, we would have "lost" because we would have had the fewest survivors.

Something had to be done. Part of the answer was to allocate funds for the construction of major shelters all over the country. Eventually many billions of tax dollars were spent. Semi-secret underground installations were built, not only in this country, but in several foreign countries as well.

The Big Secret

While the underground cities were being dug, local citizens were given a cover story. They were usually told that a major underground telephone installation was being built in their area. Ma Bell got the blame for all the furious activity. Once a "facility," as they were called, was completed, a few local people were hired to keep it clean and ready. They weren't sworn to secrecy but they weren't expected to blab about it, either. Local newspaper editors were also politely advised to ignore what was going on.

Every state has at least one of these installations. Some states have several. Each one has large dormitories with many bunks, kitchens, bathrooms, and equipment to comfortably accommodate several hundred people.

That was the problem. In case of war, millions of people would be on the move, fleeing the cities and roaming homeless over the countryside. It would be impossible to house and care for all the refugees in these underground facilities so the semi-secrecy was deemed necessary.

A scandal broke out in New Orleans because their shelter had only a few beds for black people despite the city's huge black population. (This was in the early 1960s when segregation was still being practiced.) If you were black, you were going to get nuked while all the white politicians, or "city fathers," as they sometimes call themselves, would be bowling underground.

In most cases, there are no signs pointing the way to the installations and access is by simple dirt roads. The main entrances, which consist of huge, heavy steel doors, are concealed in hillsides behind shrubbery. You have to know exactly where the facilities are and exactly how to get to them or you'll never find them. It's all part of the cunning plan to build multi-billion dollar shelters so that the people who might need them can never locate them!

There is a law, however, that these places must be open to public inspection one day each year. The public is never informed of this, though. You have to know someone who works at the installation to find out the chosen day. That's how I managed to visit the "New York Facility" a few years ago. It is located in the foothills of the Catskill Mountains and seemed like a set from a James Bond movie. You could live there quite comfortably for years without ever having to go back into the outside world.

During my travels in the 1960s, I came across several others under construction. One was near Harrisburg, Pennsylvania, not far from the notorious Three Mile Island atomic plant. Another was in the tiny state of Connecticut.

Accidents Will Happen

Occasionally one of these facilities gets into the news very briefly. Back in the 1970s, an airliner had the misfortune to crash in Virginia, not far from Washington, D.C. Firemen and rescue workers were prevented from approaching the wreck by swarms of soldiers. The plane had crashed right on top of one of these underground installations.

In the 1980s, the Japanese government began a campaign to have the island of Okinawa returned to their custody. The U.S. has claimed the island ever since we lost fifty thousand men taking it in World War II. We don't want to give it back because we have built all kinds of tunnels and underground installations on it, according to the news reports.

Recently a young man who had just been to Australia came to me and excitedly reported that he had seen a remarkable thing in the outback country, smack in the middle of the subcontinent. He had been sightseeing when a black military plane suddenly appeared and, while he watched, zoomed toward a high plateau in the center of the desert. To his amazement, a door opened in the side of the plateau and the plane flew into it. The door closed behind it. He felt that he had been an accidental witness to some top secret event.

In a way, he had. He had seen another one of our worst-kept secrets. No less an authority than *The New York Times* had spilled the beans back in the mid-1960s when they published a long article describing our plan to build a huge installation in the middle of the Australian outback.

We recruited contractors and engineers to live in that inhospitable area for at least seven years. They were permitted to take their families with them and we even planned to build a small American community there for the duration of the project. It had theaters, soda fountains and the inevitable bowling alleys.

I sent copies of the *Times*' story to correspondents in Australia and they eventually reported back that they had never heard of the project and it was never mentioned in the Australian press. But apparently the job was completed and supply planes visit it on a regular schedule.

The average Australian still doesn't know that it's there.

Holes in the Desert

Closer to home, we have been blowing holes in the Nevada desert for years with our underground atomic tests. Hundreds of atomic blasts have been set off north of Las Vegas near a place called Skull Mountain. Each one has melted a very big hole in the ground there. These holes intersect and now comprise a vast network of underground caverns.

No outsider really knows what all these caves are being used for, but they are probably being used for something. Since the underground tests have been going on for a long time, an enormous area is involved—an area big enough for a really spectacular underground city.

A fringe cult of a few dozen people has sprung up, advocating the existence of a Shaver-like underground city there in the Nevada Proving Grounds. They claim that aliens from some other planet are living there and enjoying our hospitality as they eat our strawberry ice cream and play in our bowling alleys.

However, those who understand the bureaucratic and military mentality assume that the space is just being wasted, perhaps being used to warehouse toilet seats, ashtrays, and pencil sharpeners.

Most of the backyard shelters built in the 1950s are now being used by their owners to store wine and garden tools.

The ninety-plus atomic shelters must now contain rusting, obsolete equipment and may be filled with cobwebs and bats. Meanwhile, many thousands of people are homeless in this country and are living in their cars, sleeping in parks and doorways, facing the harsh elements underclothed and underfed, while these huge facilities stand empty and forgotten.

August 1990

Something Stinks!

Take a deep breath as you stroll along a beach—any beach will do—and your nostrils will be assaulted by what smells like a mermaid's armpit. The sewers of the world are spilling into our oceans, and every time the tides come in they bring with them our old orange peels, beer cans, and discarded sweat socks. Periodically they also dump something else on our beaches—something that stinks even worse than we do.

It usually takes the form of a huge lump of grayish meat, just formless enough so that we can't quite recognize what it used to be. Holding our noses, we rush to summon the authorities and learned professors from the nearest university. The cry goes out: "A dead sea serpent has arrived on our beach!" Great mobs of curious people flock to the scene to get a good whiff of the decaying flesh while they gaze in wonder at the monster. Then the local authorities are confronted with the awesome and expensive problem of how to cart away the smelly mess.

The college professors and ichthyologists who come to probe and poke at the carcass invariably pronounce it to be the remains of a whale or a shark. For example, when a hairy, thirty-foot-long thing washed ashore at Girvan, Scotland, in September 1953, local witnesses described it as having a ten-foot, giraffe-like neck, four short legs, and a pointed tail about twelve feet long. Scottish scientists, who never bothered to go look at it, declared it to be a whale.

Forteans have another name for such things. We call them "globsters."

There have been hundreds of globster reports in the past century, from every part of the world. Some of these mounds of meat have been larger than any known whale. Some have left behind fascinating skeletons bigger than any recognizable fish. A few scientists, such as Ivan T. Sanderson and Dr. Bernard Heuvelmans, have collected and cataloged globster reports in a series of unfortunately obscure books.

Every few years a globster story manages to attract the attention of the mass media for about thirty seconds. You may recall how, in the mid-1980s, a Japanese fishing boat reported they had hauled a huge, smelly mass aboard but the stench was so bad they had to throw it back. They said it was unlike anything they had plucked from the ocean before.

If you are a regular reader of FATE, you know that many globster reports have appeared in its pages over the years. You are probably also willing to admit that our oceans are so vast and so deep that it is very possible for them to harbor all kinds of still-unknown creatures.

Mapping the Unknown

One of the world's greatest Forteans is an engineer named William Corliss, who has spent many years sifting through scientific journals and old newspapers for items about the strange and impossible things that happen all the time. He has come up with two thousand separate categories of Fortean events. Globsters are just one. There are 1,999 others, such as the odd manufactured objects that have been found deep in coal mines and rock quarries—things like steel nails, vases, and finely crafted utensils. Because they are found in strata that can be dated, some of these objects are believed to be millions of years old. A modern-looking spark plug has even been found inside a rock!

There are also many records of living things that have been found entombed in rocks. We've all heard tales of frogs that were discovered sealed within the stones of old buildings and how they came back to life and hopped away after being freed. But my personal favorite is the story of a creature that was trapped in a rock for nine million years before it was finally uncovered. Nine million years!

Pterodactyls—Not Extinct?

The story first appeared in the *Illustrated London News,* February 9, 1856. We don't know much about this publication. It may have been a Victorian version of a supermarket tabloid. According to this authoritative journal, a group of workmen were digging a tunnel in France when they blew a large block of stone apart with gunpowder and "a living being of monstrous form" staggered out. It was the size of a large goose and had wings, but the resemblance ended there.

"Its membranous wings, when spread out, measure from tip to tip three metres 22 centimeters [nearly ten feet, seven inches]," the article explained. "Its color is livid black; its skin is naked, thick and oily; its intestines only contained a colourless liquid like clear water. On reaching the light this monster gave some signs of life, by shaking its wings, but soon after expired, uttering a hoarse cry."

The creature, with its long neck, sharp teeth, and four sharp claws, was identified as an ancient pterodactyl, a gruesome relic from prehistoric times. A discovery of this kind should have elicited great excitement in the scientific journals of the period. The carcass of the beast should have been carefully stuffed and mounted in some museum for all the world to see. It had to be one of the greatest finds of the nineteenth century.

Instead, there was a stony silence. No further information appeared in British or French publications. Apparently it was just another of the journalistic hoaxes that were so common in that century. Nevertheless, the story has been repeated endlessly in all kinds of books and magazine articles, always based on that one, single source.

And people continue to see pterodactyls. There was a virtual epidemic of them in Texas in 1975 and '76 in the Brownsville area.

One was supposedly shot and then photographed by some hardy pioneers around the turn of the century. The photograph, showing a gigantic winged monster that looked something like a bat with a thyroid condition, turned up in a popular magazine in the early 1960s. It was nailed or tied to the wall of a barn, its wings spread out so you could see that it had a wingspread of twenty to thirty feet, and a group of rugged-looking men dressed like cowboys stood in front of it. They all wore proud, smug expressions. A couple of them were wearing beat-up old top hats and the caption called them "college professors" who had identified the creature as an ancient pterodactyl.

Search for a Pterodactyl

I clearly remember studying this printed photo for a long time and being quite impressed by it. But later I could not remember what magazine had published it. Other Forteans, including the late Ivan Sanderson, also remembered seeing it. We all recalled the exact same details. But none of us could remember the name of the magazine. Eventually we launched a massive search to relocate the photo. Our appeals for help were widely published and we were rewarded with many letters from all parts of the country written by people who also clearly recalled seeing it. But absolutely no one could remember where they saw it! It grew into a major mystery. Experienced researchers plowed through all kinds of periodicals, especially the men's magazines (there were over fifty such magazines in the 1950s and early 1960s). All the back issues of FATE and its numerous shabby imitators were closely scrutinized, to no avail.

The search has been going on for over twenty years now. It is amazing how many people clearly recall seeing that photo, and it is downright incredible that not one of them can remember where they saw it. Perhaps it was really on some television show, although that is very unlikely. Everyone remembers it being in a magazine and almost everyone remembers the caption about the rustic "college professors."

For some reason, the name of the *Tombstone Epitaph,* the newspaper in Tombstone, Arizona, keeps cropping up. But all of the available back issues of that noble gazette have been carefully searched. Nothing.

Do you remember seeing such a photograph? More importantly, do you remember where you saw it? If you do, I would certainly appreciate hearing from you. I'd send a generous award to anyone who can produce an actual copy of this long-lost picture. Well, maybe the award won't be so generous. Maybe it'll just be a piece of a globster and a World War II gas mask.

Or maybe just my thanks.

A.C.R.

September 1990

Future Tense

By an incredible stroke of luck, I was born in 1930, just at the beginning of the Great Depression. So I was able to enjoy all the amenities of that noble decade: kerosene lamps, outhouses, hand-operated water pumps, penny candy, and a one-room country schoolhouse with twelve pupils. There were no homeless people in those days. We had hobos who were traveling across the country looking for work. They frequently came to our kitchen door, offering to perform any chore in return for a bite to eat. They never begged, and as near as I can recall they were never refused. There were three kinds of wanderers: hobos, who would work; bums, who couldn't work; tramps, who wouldn't work. I only remember the hobos, some of whom appeared to be educated, cultured gentlemen caught up in the national economic tragedy.

Pride Amidst Poverty

The Great Depression was a time when paint was too expensive to be used on houses so the whole world had a run-down, weatherbeaten look. Everybody was poor but nobody admitted to being impoverished. To be impoverished is to be hopeless. To be impoverished is to live in a ghetto someplace and know that you will never, ever escape from it, nor will your children or grandchildren. To be young in the Great Depression meant ignoring the ugly present and looking forward to that distant land called The Future.

The Wonderful Future

Dreaming about The Future was a major industry in the 1930s. Magazines and newspapers were filled with articles about how wonderful The Future was going to be. Everyone, especially the young, talked of Tomorrow as if it were already an established fact. The hobos were wending their way from a bitter yesterday to some glorious Tomorrow just beyond the horizon.

Crystal Balls and Empty Bellies

There were public prophets in those days who saw The Future with less than crystal clarity. A 1938 poll of astrologers and soothsayers in Britain disclosed that none of them thought there would be a war. They all predicted an imminent economic recovery and a wonderful world of peace and plenty. Nobody was going to die in air raids and death camps. Nobody was going to starve to death.

Other kinds of prophets were also busily prognosticating. They were the scientists and technologists, some of whom even formed a pseudo-political party known as the Technocrats. They envisioned a vast Technocracy ruled by learned intellectuals instead of sleazy politicians and greedy opportunists.

The Fair of the Future

In 1939, the New York World's Fair was based on the theme of Tomorrow, with displays of superhighways, television (a newfangled invention), streamlined automobiles (the cars of the 1930s were mostly box-shaped clunkers), airplanes that could fly as fast as—gulp—two hundred miles an hour, and mechanical washing machines to replace the tubs and scrub boards of the era. Technocracy was just around the corner.

Hugo Gemsback, the venerable "father of science fiction," held annual press conferences to announce the new scientific wonders that were about to come. He didn't merely endorse the World's Fair—he claimed to have invented it! A Time Capsule filled with the cultural debris of 1939 was buried at the Fair with much publicity, to be dug up five thousand years hence. We were now looking ahead to a very distant future and assuming that the people of 6939 would be as interested in Dick Tracy comic strips and soda bottles as we are in ancient Egyptian vases. We had hope for a great Future.

A Mix of Good Signs and Bad

Like everyone else, I dreamed of that far-off Future even as I huddled next to a radio and listened to shortwave broadcasts from Munich, Germany. Britain's prime minister, a chap named Chamberlain, declared confidently there would be "peace in our time." The Future was assured. *Popular Science* magazine promised that all kinds of wonders were on the way. Westinghouse built a huge mechanical robot for the World's Fair. By 1960, we were told, robots would be doing all our work for us.

Then the bombs began to fall. The lights went out all over Europe. The Future had arrived.

Hope for the Future in Times of Darkness

World War II sparked our industrial imagination. While the seers and soothsayers licked their collective wounds, the new technical prophets assumed increasing prominence. The war occupied most of our attention, of course, but the popular magazines also devoted considerable space to what the world would be like in the postwar era. Once the evil Axis Powers had been defeated, the long-promised technological paradise would envelop us. Women would wear rip-proof, washable nylon stockings. (During the war years many women painted their bare legs the color of stockings.) Fragile silk, which came from the Orient, would be a thing of the past. A new flying machine called the helicopter fascinated all of us, and the technical writers of the 1940s thought it was inevitable that choppers would replace automobiles. There would be a helicopter in every garage in the postwar world.

Television had made vast technological strides in the 1930s. Germany was one of the first countries to have regular television broadcasts. In the U.S., a few experimenters and a couple of millionaires owned primitive TV receivers. At the 1939 Fair, television seemed to be a reality at last. Manufacturers of those big, ugly console radios of the 1940s cleverly included an RCA jack on the chassis of their sets, telling buyers that when TV arrived they only had to plug a picture tube into it. It was a powerful sales gimmick that worked. But no one ever did make the promised TV accessory.

Pulp magazines and Sunday supplements were caught up in another future fantasy that seemed utterly ridiculous in the 1940s. They saw rocket ships zooming into space, men walking on the moon, satellites orbiting the Earth. Even the Technocrats couldn't buy those dreams. Maybe it would happen in a few hundred years, they thought. Then again, maybe such silly notions belonged only in the Buck Rogers and Flash Gordon comic strips. Most of us would happily settle for a helicopter parked in our driveway.

Tomorrow Dies—With a Bang

While the future-mongers were peddling the wonders of Tomorrow, a small group of Hungarian physicists were enthusiastically working on a "gadget" in the New Mexico desert, a gadget that none of the astrologers and seers had anticipated. By compressing a few pounds of radioactive material with some high explosives, they could cause atoms to split. The invention of the atomic bomb changed the way we looked at The Future. We won the war, but somehow we had lost both the peace and Tomorrow.

Our Depression optimism was gone forever. Now we all sensed we were a doomed race. We were all convinced it was only a matter of time before we blew ourselves up. The children of the 1950s endured practice air raids in their schools, trained to crawl under their desks in a silly and hopeless effort to escape sizzling radioactivity.

The Future wasn't a positive hope anymore. People feared it. Professional prophets and seers prattled on about one single theme—when and how the Third World War would come and consume us all. Dates were set for The End...again and again.

The Technocrats faded from view. Television, that invention with so much promise, rotted our minds and turned our children into illiterate, monosyllabic cretins. The Future we dreamed about in the 1930s and early '40s came and went with uneasy suddenness. One generation drove huge, comfortable, gas-guzzling, tail-finned automobiles. The next generation was driving tiny, toylike putt-putts that cost five times as much as the old gas guzzlers.

There were more wars, some seeming to have no other purpose than to kill people. We flew to the Moon. But the Future seemed to be short-circuited. Our children grew up terrified, convinced they were eventually going to be fried in an atomic war. In the 1970s, greed and selfishness replaced the old Golden Rule. There was no wonderful Future in our hearts and dreams. We knew now that there would never be a helicopter in every garage. Young people did not discuss Tomorrow. They talked only about survival.

In the early 1980s, there was a revival of interest in the prophecies of Nostradamus. It began in France and then swept the world. A thousand interpretations and misinterpretations of his predictions appeared. Hundreds of years ago he had prophesied the end of the world in 1999...July, to be exact. Now everyone nodded and glumly agreed. We were living in the End Times. Young people had no interest in Tomorrow. They cared only about enjoying the present.

Somehow, there was something almost comforting about living in the end times. It took away the worry and the uncertainty. It also took away the responsibility for Tomorrow—the responsibility that all previous generations had felt.

We have lost the hope of a wonderful Future, and there is a darkness hovering over the 1990s that is of our own manufacture. Every crystal ball is murky. The Future is behind us. Will we be able to regain it? I don't know.

But the world is changing. Walls are crumbling and the old ways are being pushed aside. Perhaps we will find the Wonderful Future once again. It must come from our hearts.

October 1990

Kooky Spooks

Ghosts are the silliest non-people I know.

They hang out in drafty graveyards and old, broken-down houses. Stairways are another of their favorite haunts. They are often seen floating up and down old staircases, not because they are trying to go somewhere—they have nowhere to go, it seems—but because stairs are their natural habitats.

Bats prefer belfries and caves. Ghosts like stairways. It may be as simple as that.

When they aren't popping out from behind tombstones or trotting up and down stairs, ghosts are also fond of peering out of windows and posing for photographers.

As soon as the camera was invented back in the 1800s, our shy, ethereal friends were turning up unexpectedly in family photos. The evidence suggests that whenever a group of people gathered in front of a school or manse to have their picture taken, the neighborhood ghost would part the curtains on a window and peek out just as the photographer opened his shutter. Think of how many of these pictures have been published over the years. You may have several on your own bookshelf. There are your old school classmates self-consciously staring into the lens while behind them, in a window on the seond floor of the empty schoolhouse, there is the pale, expressionless visage of a long-gone teacher or a celebrated local mass murderer.

Ghosts love to have their pictures taken.

Visitors to Graceland, the home of the late Elvis Presley, have sworn that they have seen Elvis—the King himself—staring out the windows. There are pictures in circulation to back up these claims.

More Elusive Bogeys

Ghosts may like to pose for their portraits, but other creatures of the night are more reluctant. Although thousands have tried, very few adventurous photographers have managed to film the elusive Bigfoot or his Oriental relative, the Abominable Snowman. A few pictures do exist, of course, but they are mostly indistinct and mired in controversy. Tall, hairy creatures desperately in need of a bath and a good delousing just don't linger around second-story windows.

Equally shy are our freshwater sea serpents. Like Bigfoot, they don't wait around for photographers to load their cameras. Since 1933, hundreds, sometimes thousands of summer tourists have gathered at Loch Ness in Scotland in the hopes of snapping dear old Nessie. But Nessie has demonstrated a curious talent for turning up in parts of the lake where there are no cameras. The few pictures and movie films that have been taken are oddly inconclusive.

Across the decades, countless numbers of hobbyists have avidly collected ghost pictures. Great debates on their authenticity have been held in all the world capitols. An endless stream of eyewitnesses have vouched for the pictures while skeptics and believers have screamed at each other and, in a few instances, punched each other out. Another group who call themselves "cryptozoologists" happily clutch their plaster-of-paris footprints and all-too-rare photos of smelly Bigfoot and horny-headed sea serpents proclaiming the critters real but camera-shy. Even Royal Air Force camera experts have joined the fray and given some Nessie films their stamp of approval, much to the delight of the Loch Ness Tourist Board.

What has all this sound and fury proven? Not very much.

Elvis may really be peeking out his bedroom window, but only the Elvis fans seem to care. Nessie, Bigfoot, and all their ugly brethren have escaped capture, and even those eyewitnesses who have gotten a really good look at them find it difficult to convince journalists and scientists.

Pictures by the Pound

While many books have been filled with pictures of bogeymen, monsters, and nasty crawling or swimming things that manage to hide from us part of the time, the most photographed phenomena on this planet are also the least understood and most ignored. Since 1896, hundreds of thousands—perhaps even millions—of photos of unidentified flying objects have been taken. Certainly many thousands of these pictures have been published in magazines and newspapers all over the world. Yet, incredibly, nobody has ever attempted to collect these pictures on a large scale and carry out a comprehensive, systematic study of them! This total lack of interest may be a more intriguing phenomenon than the objects themselves.

The much-maligned U.S. Air Force didn't even bother to maintain a good file of UFO photos. Newsmen and scientists who have examined the official photo files have been dismayed by their disarray. Various UFO hobbyists have made a sincere effort to collect published pictures, usually with a total disregard for the copyright laws. In New Jersey, August C. Roberts has kept a massive file of UFO photos for decades. A Hungarian refugee in New York, Colman von Keviczky, has earned an international reputation with his huge collection. If you visit a UFO convention and see a display of blowups of UFOs, chances are they are from his collection. Yet these two gentlemen have barely scratched the surface.

How to Get Rich

The now almost-forgotten Great UFO Wave of the 1960s produced many thousands of new pictures, most of which were doomed to end up in scrapbooks and boxes in attics. Some of these amateur photographers figured they could get rich by peddling their UFO photos to major magazines so they made expensive trips to New York City, clutching their precious negatives. Many of these people ended up in my office, totally dismayed. They had been stunned to learn that UFO pictures were not highly regarded. The wire services and photo agencies offered them ten dollars if they would sign away all rights to the photos. *Life* magazine, then a preeminent weekly picture magazine, was more generous. They would pay up to fifty dollars for a really good color photo.

Today, almost a generation later, an outstanding UFO photo might bring the princely sum of twenty-five dollars—if you can find a buyer.

Why is this?

The answer is that UFO photos are as common as stuffed owls. For every published picture, there are probably five hundred others that will never be printed. Once in a great while a UFO photographer does hit the jackpot, of course. Edward Walters of Gulf Breeze, Florida, is a good example. The authenticity of his pictures was endorsed by Dr. Bruce Macabbee and many others. "Mr. Ed," as he is called, managed to sell his photos and his story for six figures. Yet the Gulf Breeze photos are less impressive than many of those that have crossed my desk over the years.

My usual advice to the photographers was that they should just give copies to the various civilian UFO organizations.

Does Anybody Care?

Cryptozoologists and ghost hunters would be absolutely delirious with delight if they had only a fraction of the photographic evidence available to the amateur ufologists.

Look magazine once did an issue of nothing but UFO pictures. Imagine an entire issue of Nessie or Bigfoot photos. Those controversies would be ended forever. It is probably possible to collect and publish a six-volume set of UFO photos. Would that finish the endless, often mindless UFO debate? Probably not.

In the past year, we have all witnessed extensive media debate over the stealth bomber. Would it fly? Was it even real? The manufacturers of this multi-billion-dollar boondoggle finally wheeled out a big, black plane that managed to take off and lumber around the airport with its wheels hanging down. Aviation experts studied photos of this contraption and gleefully pointed out that the wheels couldn't retract because they had been lifted from a Boeing airliner!

Why don't these same aviation experts bother to study the massive UFO photo files and figure out the basic characteristics of "flying saucers"? In its way, the stealth bomber and its attending controversy is just a variation on our old UFO theme. First it was a legend. Then it was a massive pile of junk that could only taxi up and down a runway.

Then it became a reality by actually flying—although it didn't do it very well. Pictures of it were widely printed.

Now it is returning to the status of a legend. Soon it will be forgotten. A close-up photo of a stealth bomber is worth about twenty-five dollars. But in the early days of the controversy, a British photographer positioned himself at a gas station near the airport and took some pictures that earned him a pretty penny.

If an immodest Bigfoot should suddenly pose for tourists in Yellowstone National Park, his market value would also collapse.

We live in an age when technological miracles are boring and UFOs have been around for so long and in such great numbers that nobody cares anymore. If one landed on the White House lawn, it would probably get a parking ticket and be towed away. Nobody would even bother to take a picture.

ED.L.

November 1990

The Magnificent Loners

Back in 1893, a sealing ship happened to wander below the Antarctic Circle and blundered upon a place now called Seymour Island. It was a bleak, windswept chunk of ice and snow off the eastern coast of the Palmer Peninsula. In those days, that part of the world was almost completely unknown and uninhabited. Yet, according to Captain C. A. Larson of the sealer *Jason*, Seymour Island was speckled with curious little upright cones wrought from clay, with a clay ball sitting atop each pillar.

"These had the appearance of having been made by human hands," Captain Larson reported in his log. The structures seemed to be evidence that a human being had been there in that awful place and, perhaps out of desperation and loneliness, he had tried to leave something behind using the only materials available. He may have been a shipwrecked sailor from some forgotten whaling ship or an Indian from South America whose canoe had been caught in some fierce storm or ocean current.

Our beleaguered little oasis in space is dotted with small monuments to man's presence. If you climb Mount Everest you will find the summit littered with old tin cans, oxygen bottles, and tattered flags. If you dive twenty thousand feet below the ocean's surface you will find stacks of man-made debris and wreckage. On islands even more remote than Seymour Island you are likely to find stone ruins from forgotten civilizations. We like to leave our mark behind—even if it is only a carving on a tree or a pillar of clay.

Watts Towers

Some men have spent years of their lives preparing their monuments. Their work is everywhere. In the heart of Los Angeles, the famous Watts Towers remind us of the humble workman who spent his evenings and weekends fashioning towers out of cement and broken pottery for thirty years while his neighbors shook their heads and pointed their fingers.

The neighbors are all gone now, but the towers still stand (although local bureaucrats have been trying to have them torn down).

One lone Indian, isolated and abandoned, could have created the lines on the Nazca Plain in South America. They were made by simply scraping away the surface dirt, so one man could have accomplished the job easily—although there are some who like to fantasize that the lines were the work of a whole race eagerly trying to communicate with visitors from outer space.

The largest man-made pyramid in the world sits deep in China. Geologists now suspect that one of the mountains in the Andes in South America was built by men hauling dirt to it in baskets over many generations!

In Europe, hundreds of stone castles still stand as testimony to man's industry. Historical records tell us that some of the great castles of the Rhine Valley took as long as three hundred years to construct and were the work of many generations of villagers.

The Coral Castle

He was only four feet, eleven inches tall and probably weighed about 120 pounds soaking wet. We would never have even noticed his brief sojourn on Earth if he had not left behind a remarkable structure which still attracts thousands of visitors every year. It's the Coral Castle in Florida.

His name was Edward Leedskalnin and he emigrated to America from Latvia in the 1920s. After working at various odd jobs he settled in Florida, which, in those days, was largely a thinly populated swamp. It was a land of snakes, bugs, alligators, and high humidity. Ed arrived with an old truck and a broken heart. (His young girlfriend in Latvia had dumped him.) Soon the truck was broken, too, and he dismantled it to build a bicycle from its parts.

For the next three decades, he would labor alone in the swamps, somehow quarrying huge slabs of coral stone and transporting them over two miles to the site of his dream castle. Some of the stones weighed as much as nine tons, and how he managed to move them is still a mystery. His few neighbors never caught him in the act of actually working the coral or building his strange structure.

First, he built a tower which he used as his living quarters. Around that he constructed a high wall of coral, making a kind of stone fortress. One entrance through the wall was a huge stone slab, weighing several tons, which he somehow mounted on a pivot so it could be pushed open with one finger. No one has ever figured out how the thin little man managed to get the stone into place and so perfectly balanced without any heavy equipment or sophisticated tools.

When the Coral Castle itself was completed, Ed went on to sculpt huge pieces of stone furniture, including a large table, several chairs, a coral bed, and even a twenty-five-foot obelisk. None of these pieces display any tool marks or other clues as to how he managed to fashion them, transport them, and move them into place.

When an occasional awed visitor would ask for his secret, Ed would just smile enigmatically and say that he used the same techniques that had been used to build the pyramids.

Hardly a satisfactory answer.

Move the Whole Thing

Once the Coral Castle was finished, Ed decided to move it closer to a main highway so he could draw more tourists. That must have been another massive undertaking, for the whole thing was moved several miles—stone by stone. Tourists on their way to Key West began to stop in larger and larger numbers. Ed charged a small admission fee and was able to devote more time to his study of magnetism, his favorite pursuit. From the papers and equipment he left behind, it is apparent that his knowledge of magnetism was on the level of a high-school physics student. It is very unlikely that he knew some great secret that enabled him to use magnetism to move the coral around.

Another striking fact about the castle and sculptures is that Ed had no apparent artistic ability at all. Everything was crudely formed. There was no aesthetic plan to any of it. He probably worked without even the simplest of patterns or blueprints. None of the stones were "dressed" (polished or smoothed out) and they were loosely fitted together.

Ed himself lived on a very simple level, existing primarily on canned sardines. His diet was not very nourishing and he slowly starved to death in 1951, thus ending what must have been a life of great hardship and unimaginable loneliness, a life that had been spent in an inhospitable swamp tediously hacking away at great stone blocks.

But it was not a wasted life. The Coral Castle has brought pleasure and wonder to millions of people in the last forty years.

Secrets of the Ages

Learned scientists and archaeologists have been debating for years about the pyramids of Egypt, often claiming that it must have taken hundreds of thousands of slaves to build those great structures. All kinds of fanciful theories have been promoted as solutions. However, when we look at the modern wonders of the Watts Towers, the Coral Castle, the Nazca lines, and the many other works of lone individuals using only primitive tools, the pyramids lose much of their mystery.

Instead of great armies of slaves, it is quite possible that a few Ed Leedskalnins could have erected the Great Pyramid in a very short time. Maybe there was just one family of professional pyramid builders who toured the world, pausing in Great Britain to set up Stonehenge, then moving on to Mexico, China, and a thousand other places to leave their mark.

Even on the Moon we have left behind proof of our existence. Our astronauts didn't fashion any clay pillars with balls on top, but they did abandon an expensive four-wheeled vehicle, some flags and cameras, and even a golf ball. Some future race, as yet unborn, will certainly be baffled when they find those things there.

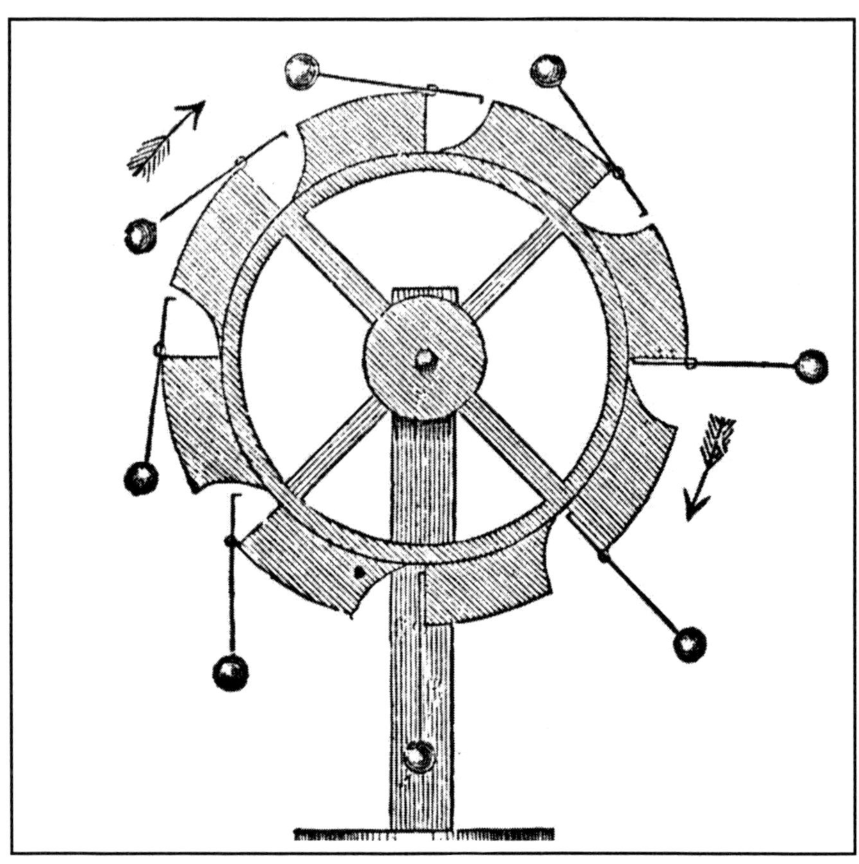

December 1990

Something for Nothing

Despite his illustrious name, John Keely is remembered as a rotten, lowdown swindler of wealthy widows—hardly a fitting epitaph for a man who claimed to have invented a machine that would revolutionize the industrial world. It performed amazing wonders in his laboratory, but Keely never managed to get it onto the market. He just kept raising more money. Some say he peddled as much as five million dollars in stocks in his ill-fated Keely Motor Company...an astounding sum in the 1890s when he was at his peak.

Without an apparent source of power, the Keely apparatus was capable of bending heavy bars of steel in front of skeptical scientists, engineers, and industrialists. Keely used tuning forks and musical instruments to set his machinery in motion, and his frequent demonstrations made him one of the most controversial people of the Victorian Age. But after he passed away in 1898, disgruntled investors ripped his home apart and found a curious system of pipes, valves, and spherical tanks hidden in the walls and floorboards. They concluded that Keely had somehow used compressed air to power his wonderful machines. He had presumably exploited one of humanity's oldest dreams—the dream of obtaining "free energy," of getting something for nothing, of perpetual motion.

The search for perpetual motion probably began soon after a cave man invented the wheel. At least one man, a German clock maker who called himself "Orffyreus," reputedly developed the world's first successful self-propelled wheel around 1715 after building some three hundred failures. To prove that it worked, it was sealed in a room in a castle in Hesse after being set in motion. When the room was reopened two months later, the wheel was still spinning merrily by itself. Assorted professors and authorities examined it and wrote about it but "Orffyreus" eventually smashed the wheel to pieces and that was the end of it. It is generally assumed that it was driven by some hidden clockwork mechanism. We'll never know because the inventor got miffed when the government tried to tax it. Governments haven't changed much since. Nor have perpetual motion inventors.

Congress Gets Swindled

Mr. Garabed Giragossian, an Armenian, appealed to President Woodrow Wilson in 1917, asking for a chance to prove the merits of his "free energy" machine. Instead of taxing the device, President Wilson set up a congressional committee to investigate the claims. Within a year, Giragossian was one of the most famous men in America. Senators, congressmen, military officials, and learned scientists all made a serious study of the heavy revolving wheel, and thousands of dollars were spent on preparing official reports. Eventually, however, a young engineer realized that it was really just a flywheel turned by a small, battery-driven motor. Once the heavy wheel was set in motion, the little motor was able to keep it going indefinitely. Congress had been swindled. So what else is new?

Most perpetual motion inventors find they are battling gravity, friction, and inertia. Elaborate systems of moving weights, a favorite with free energy enthusiasts, must eventually cease moving because of these factors. Early astronauts returned from space orbits with some exciting news, though. Friction seemed to disappear when they were in a weightless condition. A thousand lights flashed in a thousand heads at this news, and several NASA subcontractors went to work on perpetual motion devices. Little gadgets that would only work in space were actually devised, along with things like the "fuel cells" that supplied power in new ways. But no full-fledged, outer-space, frictionless motor was ever developed. Nor has NASA tested any of the old shifting-weight mechanisms of the early inventors which might actually work in space.

The Great Water Hoax

While Mr. Giragossian was entertaining Congress, a man named John Andrews was performing amazing demonstrations at the Brooklyn Naval Yard. He would pour some green powder into a tank of water and use it to run a gasoline engine. Naval officials were flabbergasted, but suspicious. Andrews and his green powder disappeared for several years. He turned up again in the 1930s, this time demonstrating his green powder for the National Bureau of Standards. Two years later, he was mysteriously murdered. His story has been told over and over again in the vast literature on "suppressed inventions," along with the tales of marvelous carburetors that enable you to get one hundred or more miles to a gallon of gas, and so on.

The old water-to-gasoline story still reappears every few years and a number of people have turned a fast buck with it. Substances such as acetone will actually run a combustion engine for a short period. Of course, they will also wreck the engine very quickly. During the gas shortage of 1973, a man named Guido Franchi appeared in the Midwest and held public demonstrations of his magic powder, accompanied by considerable publicity. A few ounces of the stuff seemed to turn water into gasoline. He said he learned to make the powder from "the Black Eagles," a group of spacemen who, he said, live on the planet Neptune. While this claim endeared him to the UFO community, it didn't make much of an impression on the bankers he approached with his offer to sell his secret formula for a mere ten million dollars. After being threatened with jail, Mr. Franchi disappeared from view.

Incidentally, the P-51 "Thunderbolt" fighter plane of World War II really did fly on water—sort of. When the pilot needed extra power he pulled a lever in the cockpit and water was sprayed into the hot engine where it turned into steam instantly and gave the pistons an added kick.

It is possible to devise an automobile engine that will really run on water. You just need a converter to separate the hydrogen and oxygen into gases and regulate the mix. A few inventors have, in fact, attempted to build such a motor. Usually, they managed to blow themselves up. Hydrogen and oxygen can make a very explosive combination. The Germans did use hydrogen peroxide (H_2O_2) as a fuel during the Second World War. But it did a lot of damage to the engines because it causes rapid oxidization.

Perpetual Electricity

Nikola Tesla, the great Yugoslav genius who discovered alternating current, was convinced that electricity could be drawn from the air, thus giving us an unending source of free energy. After all, the spinning Earth with its natural magnetic field is really a giant electrical dynamo. But no one has ever found a way to tap this great energy source.

Many basement tinkerers have tried to perfect self-running electric motors without much success. There was Lester Hendershot who, in the 1920s, accidentally built a motor that seemed to produce amazing amounts of power. Unfortunately, Hendershot was not a trained engineer. He didn't know how his motor worked and was unable to build more of them. In the 1930s, Dr. Thomas Henry Moray of Salt Lake City successfully demonstrated an electrical device that seemed to work on some free energy principle. In the process, he also managed to invent the Moray Valve, which was really the first transistor. It was a key component of his free energy generator and the Patent Office rejected his application because transistors were not known at the time (1936). Bell Laboratories would not develop the modern transistor for another twenty years. Dr. Moray and his inventions landed in the dustbin of history.

Another designer of an extraordinary electric motor, Edwin V. Gray, surfaced in the 1950s with a demonstrable "EMS motor" that seemed to be the answer to all our energy needs. The Los Angeles district attorney took a different view, however, and raided his offices in 1974, confiscating his records and plans. Years of legal problems followed, and Mr. Gray's motor joined Dr. Moray's.

The basic problem seems to have a basic solution. If you want to build a perpetual motion machine of your own, you need only hook a generator to an electric motor. The motor will run the generator and the generator will produce the electricity to keep the motor going. Uncounted thousands have tried to do this, but for some reason the motor always consumes more electricity than the generator can produce. Giragossian's wheel needed small amounts of energy to run its little electric motor. Hendershot's machine needed a couple of flashlight batteries. John Keely needed a tank of hot air.

Solar power may provide the ultimate answer. Photoelectric cells drawing energy from the sun are now running experimental automobiles, airplanes, and space satellites. We are slowly learning to harness natural forces, and perhaps some amateur inventor in some basement or garage workshop will eventually hit upon the missing link that will put all the oil companies out of business.

January 1991

You've Got to Be Taught

Why is it that nearly all famous magicians froth at the mouth when you mention psychic phenomena or parapsychology? In fact, I have rarely met any magicians—famous or unknown—who have not scowled at the kind of things you read about in every issue of this magazine. They suffer from a stupefying, totally irrational prejudice against anything and everything deemed paranormal. Alternatively, they will blindly accept the most ridiculous pontifications of modern science. What ails these people anyway?

Since I have been an avid magician from the age of seven and have even written books about sleight-of-hand and the conjurer's art, and since I once toured the country performing a very inept magic act, I am qualified to bore you with the details of one of magic's best-kept secrets. Show this article to your skeptical magician friends and watch them fume and turn purple.

As with any racial, religious, or political prejudice, the fear of the paranormal has a deeply rooted emotional cause. You may be afraid of snakes because when you were a small child and encountered a harmless garden snake your mother or father (probably your mother) stomped on it with revulsion while screaming, "Kill it! Kill it!" This led you to conclude that snakes were loathsome creatures that should be destroyed on sight. You probably grew up with a really rotten attitude toward things that were creepy and crawlie.

Magicians are caught up in this same kind of attitude, stemming from their early years. Most magicians—and I have known a great many—first became involved in the subject when they were very young, just as I did. They become eager readers of magic books, starting with simple books on card tricks and basic magic. But by the time they reach their early teens they are reading the biographies of famous magicians and the more advanced books on stage illusions, the history of magic, and so on. Their immature minds, untrained to be critical, are very, very impressionable.

Unfortunately, the magical literature is largely written by egomaniacs who wallow in all kinds of delusions about the world and their place in it. Their emotionalism easily rubs off onto their young readers. One of the most common threads of anger and hate running through this literature is a complete misinterpretation of all things psychic. So the magic books have the same kind of effect as books on, say, racist themes or, alas, UFOs. The younger reader is not able to evaluate what he is reading so he accepts this trash and it becomes part of the fabric of his being.

A learned friend of mine once observed that you should never try to argue with a Marxist or a Hindu because they think they have an answer for everything in their belief system. We might add magicians to that category.

Houdini's Contribution

There is little doubt that Harry Houdini launched the modern anti-psychic bias in the magical literature. During the last years of his life (he died on Halloween, 1926), he campaigned vigorously against psychics and spirit mediums, receiving considerable publicity, in the process. Following World War I, there had been a great revival in spiritualism as bereaved wives and parents of soldiers killed in battle tried to make contact with their lost ones. This trend led to the development of a minor industry in bogus mediums who exploited the pain and sorrow of the bereft families.

Houdini was a master at self-promotion. That's why he's still remembered more than sixty years after his death. In the heyday of vaudeville he was the top-drawing performer, filling theaters because of his publicity stunts. My friend, the late Walter Gibson, knew Houdini well and once confided to me that Houdini was really not a very good magician. He was a showman—a kind of P. T. Barnum of magic. A small man with a heavy European accent, Houdini convinced the world that he was a great escape artist.

His show was absurd by today's standards. He would be trussed up with ropes and chains, then locked into a box or a tank of water. The curtains would close and the orchestra would begin to play. The audience would sit there for thirty minutes staring at the curtain, waiting for Houdini to make his escape. Actually, Houdini would usually free himself in the first two or three minutes and then sit behind the curtain and read a newspaper, waiting for the audience to get anxious and nervous.

Part of the Houdini legend is that he began to visit spirit mediums after the death of his beloved mother but he encountered so many frauds and phonies that he decided to begin his anti-psychic crusade. The truth is somewhat more mundane than that.

The Search for Spirits

Vaudeville had been the nation's chief entertainment for about fifty years when, in the 1920s, movies became serious competition. The vaudeville theaters—and there were thousands of them—began to suffer. Even headliners like Houdini began to play to half-empty theaters. His once highly effective publicity stunts no longer worked. A whole generation had grown up watching him wriggle out of straitjackets and plunge into icy rivers in heavy manacles. He had even made a few motion pictures which only contributed further to his decline. As a movie actor he came across as a glowering cornball.

So, almost in desperation, Houdini began his heavily publicized attack against spiritualists, mediums, and psychics. The campaign was so successful that other magicians joined in.

Exposing the trickery of the fake mediums became an essential part of every new magic book. Young magicians were led to believe that all psychic phenomena was based upon easily explainable hoaxes, frauds, and manipulations.

After Houdini's death, his forays into the world of séances were turned into legend. Other magicians, eager to gain publicity, tried to follow his example. Some, such as the late Joseph Dunninger, even managed to build fruitful careers by doing so. Scores of magazine articles, newspaper stories and books continued to appear, all extolling Houdini's virtues and adding to his growing legend. Even today, at least one new book about the escape artist appears every year. Sixty years after his death, his reputation continues to grow.

Every young magician devours the Houdini books and dreams of becoming a famous ghostbuster like him. They grow up to be passionately biased, having been effectively brainwashed by the mostly unfounded, even irresponsible, trash they absorbed in their youth. The authors of these books don't bother to examine the now vast literature on parapsychology and psychic phenomena. They are somehow stuck in the 1920s.

Where Have All the Ghosts Gone?

Exposing fake mediums is not so easy as it was in Houdini's day.

Thousands of eager magicians are constantly combing the country in search of séances…a vain pursuit since spiritualism has been on the decline in the U.S. for many years, and very few people come forward with what were once considered outrageous psychic claims.

While parapsychology and the scientific study of the paranormal have come a very long way since Houdini's period, the magicians are still locked into their now-antiquated beliefs—or disbeliefs. They have been passed by and that must make them even madder.

For a few years in the 1950s, spook shows enjoyed a certain popularity. These were road shows operated by professional magicians that held fake séances on stage and produced ghosts and monsters for paying audiences. The best-known spook show magician was a man named Bill Neff, but there were many others including Uri Geller and James Randi. Quite a few of the young magicians of the '50s got their training performing in spook shows. Even though audience interest in the fake séances disappeared a generation ago, some of these magicians still persistently promote the old anti psychic nonsense.

Occasionally you see them on TV talk shows babbling the fiction about how "millions" of people are being taken in by fake psychics who con money from little old ladies. Articles written in this vein continue to appear in the numerous magazines and newsletters devoted to magic.

This returns us to our original question: Why do magicians hate psychic phenomena? Basically, they think that they can repeat Houdini's success with the ploy. Actually, some of them are too dumb and too brainwashed to recognize that the fraud and fakery of Houdini's time is a thing of the past. It would be more useful for them to study the accounting wizardry of the Pentagon and find out how a toilet seat can cost six hundred dollars.

That's real magic!

February 1991

The Big Cultural Shock

If you indulge in astral projection, you know the shock of traveling far out into space and looking back at the little blue lump that is your home. When viewed in the vast blackness of deep space, the Earth doesn't seem to amount to very much. It appears to be just another mass of gases and fluids adrift in the cosmos.

If you are not an astral projectionist, you probably suffered the shock of recognition in the late 1960s when our satellites—and later our astronauts—began sending back photographs of our crisis-ridden planet. For the first time in human history we really understood our communal plight. As philosopher-scientist Buckminster Fuller observed, we are all passengers on a spaceship largely composed of nitrogen, oxygen, and hydrogen. In a sense we are all prisoners and, except for the astral projectionists among us, are doomed to live out our lives confined to this tiny corner of the Milky Way orbiting a pathetic little star.

For many years, a framed copy of the NASA Earth photo hung above my desk. It served as a constant reminder of the humility that was part of being a minor lifeform on a trivial planet trapped in a mediocre solar system. When my earthly affairs would seem to assume monstrously important proportions I would look at that picture and tell myself that not even the great city I lived in was big enough to register on the film.

Millions of other Tellurians—or Earthlings—reacted to the same picture in much the same way. It was hung on thousands of walls and curbed uncounted egos. We were all in the same fix. We were not only all stuck on this same island in space, but we were responsible for the awesome job of keeping it habitable.

Those photos of the "Earthrise" taken from the Moon may have been the most important pictures ever made. When they were circulated and published worldwide, the entire human race suffered that shock of recognition.

Shape Up or Ship Out

For thousands of years, human beings liked to believe that the Earth was the center of the universe and that the Sun and stars revolved around it. That was a comforting view of the cosmos. The Earth seemed enormous, flat, and almost unending. Now, in the twentieth century, we know more about our planet and ourselves than all of the generations who preceded us. What's more, we are in full communication with each other for the first time in history. Radio, television, and aviation are bringing us all together. We share a common awareness that would have been inconceivable a mere hundred years ago.

Not satisfied with our puny triumphs, we engaged in mass loneliness. We stood in the fields and deserts and gazed at the night skies. Were we alone—or were there others like us somewhere out there beyond the stars? We began to dream of other worlds, perhaps better than our own. We longed for companionship with remote beings and their civilizations.

We began to build machines that could leave our planet.

We constructed high powered radar sets and elaborate radio receivers that could intercept signals from far places.

For the past thirty years we have searched for some trace of life in some other corner of the Milky Way. While our radar beams poked at the planets in our solar system our astronomers listened to their radios and squinted through their telescopes. We hoped for a sign, any small indication that there was somebody else out there. The cost of this great search was mind-boggling. The thought that we might be alone was intolerable.

An ugly thing was also happening during those thirty years, something we had never expected or counted upon. Our convoluted civilization was collapsing inwardly upon itself like a black hole. The many worlds contained within our world were colliding and collapsing. Humanity was like a trapped animal desperately chewing off its own foot.

A Golden Age had gripped us for a full century, between 1848 and 1948. It was an age of industrialization, invention, social reform, music, literature, and art. We never expected it to end. When it ended, it did so in such a slow and subtle way that most of us didn't even notice. Yet now we find ourselves in a post-industrial age, living on the crumbs of a dying culture. Our search for other worlds and other universes is fading, too. The answer has been found. There are no patterned radio waves being beamed at us from afar. There are no entities out there seeking contact with us. We may be more alone than we ever dared to imagine. This blue orb may be all there is. We have become like a shipwreck victim on a remote island, scanning the horizon for ships that will never come.

Search for Renewal

In the past, religion often came to the rescue in times of trial. When we were beset by horrible plagues, wars, and great natural disasters, we sought supernatural help and solace. In this technological era, a new kind of religion sprang up.

The worldwide flying saucer cults of the 1940s and 1950s promised an interstellar brotherhood and salvation from those distant worlds that we hoped existed. As the Bible had promised in a slight variation two thousand years earlier, the kindly space people were going to rescue a selected few when the time came. There was always hope, it seemed, of outside intervention.

Then, in the 1980s, the slow and terrible realization of our loneliness, our abandonment in the void, began to pall over us. We sent out more probes into space. Voyager I and Voyager II hurtled past the other planets, sending back television photos of Jupiter and Saturn and their moons.

In the 1950s, millions still believed that lifeforms like ourselves resided on those hostile bodies. Now all the dreams of the saucer cultists were smashed. We were lonelier than ever.

The Last Martians

A pixel is not a female pixie. It is one tiny, electronic dot on a television screen. Video images are made up of such dots by the many thousands. When Voyager II reached the outer edge of our solar system in 1990, it turned its camera back towards the sun and snapped one final picture of the blue planet that had been its base of origin. Now that planet was reduced to less than one pixel! Look closely at your own television set and pick out one tiny dot. That represents the Earth's size within its own solar system. It is smaller than a grain of sand.

The "Earthrise" pictures had placed our world in a new perspective. Now the Voyager picture put us into proper context with the universe. We were 0.12 of a single pixel.

From another galaxy, our Sun would probably be even smaller and we would not be visible at all.

A famous NASA scientist who, incidentally, is also a Pulitzer Prize winner, phrased it this way in a recent newspaper article: "What is the glory and triumph of the greatest conquerors and builders of empires? They were the momentary masters of a fraction of a blue dot. Our posturings, our imagined self-importance, the delusion that we have some privileged position in the universe, are challenged by this point of pale light. Our planet is a lonely speck in the vast and enveloping cosmic dark.

"It is the only world known so far to harbor life. There is nowhere else, at least in the known future, to which our species can migrate. It is a lovely, fragile, finite little planet. But its importance lies only, I think, in what we make of it." (Dr. Carl Sagan in *Parade*, September 9, 1990.)

In his classic novel *The Martian Chronicles*, Ray Bradbury describes how Tellurians on Mars look at their reflections in a Martian river and suddenly realize that they are now the only Martians. We have looked into deep space in the same way and discovered that there may be no space people out there. We may be the only space people—passengers on an organic spaceship.

It is a chilling prospect, but all the biologists, anthropologists and evolutionists may be right when they insist that this is the only place in the universe to support the birth and existence of life. This little blue dot may be all there is and our loneliness, our hunger for intergalactic social intercourse, may never be satisfied. We must direct all of our attention and all of our energy to preserving this solitary oasis in the black coldness of the universe. Keeping the Earth alive may be our one and only mission. Thus far we have done a rather poor job of it.

March 1991

The Thunderbird Rises from the Ashes

That missing Thunderbird pterodactyl photo is still missing. My recent plea in the pages of FATE for information on the publication of a picture of a dead pterodactyl nailed to a beam produced more than twenty responses from readers who said they, too, remembered seeing it sometime between 1940 and 1960. Unfortunately, each correspondent remembered a different source. Some thought it had appeared in a magazine advertisement—possibly in *Life* or another major publication—in which case it could have been a staged phony designed to sell beer or cigarettes. Others thought it must have been in a men's magazine, but there were more than fifty such magazines in the early 1960s. (We haven't found a volunteer willing to struggle through all those girlie photos in search of it.) A Canadian writer was sure he had seen it on TV.

People have approached me at lectures, in TV studios, and at conventions to inform me that they also remembered it exactly as I had described it in FATE. It is gratifying that so many have a vivid memory of seeing it, but it is disheartening that nobody can remember where they saw it. One cynic even suggested that years from now everyone who read my column will claim that they also saw the picture, as the memory does play tricks on all of us.

An Earlier Search

A gentleman in Pennsylvania passed along some interesting clippings about his father's search for the elusive Thunderbird a generation ago. His name was Robert Lyman and he published numerous articles and books about the weird and the unknown. He thought the picture had appeared in *True*

Western magazine sometime in the 1950s. In his book, *Amazing Indeed*, the following appeared:

"Fred Murray lived in Westfield, Tioga County. He said that in 1892 he saw a flock of giant birds in Dent's Run, Cameron County. He described them as being like buzzards but much larger, with a wingspread of sixteen feet or more. The report made news at the time. An ornithologist from Pittsburgh came to Murray's lumber camp to observe them. He said similar birds had been seen in remote parts of West Virginia and Kentucky.

"About 1900, two prospectors shot and carried into Tombstone, Arizona, one of these birds. When nailed against the wall of the Tombstone Epitaph building its wingspread measured thirty-six feet. A photograph showed six men standing under the bird with outstretched arms touching. One of them said: 'Shucks, there is no such bird, never was and never will be.' I saw that picture in a daily paper. Many other persons member seeing it. No one has able to find it in recent years. Two copies were at Hammersley Fork only a few years ago. One burned in a home. The other was taken away by strangers."

Author Lyman described one of his personal sightings in the book. "About 1940 I saw a huge bird I am certain was a Thunderbird," he wrote. "It was on the ground in the center of the Sheldon Road, about two miles north of Coudersport, Pennsylvania. It was brownish in color. Legs and neck were short. It was between three and four feet tall and stood upright like a very large vulture. When I was about 150 feet away it raised to fly. It was plain to see its wingspread was equal to the width of the roadbed, which I measured and found to be twenty-five feet. I will concede it may have been twenty feet but no less. The wings were very narrow, not over one foot wide.

"How could such a bird fly through the wood? The bird I saw could have gone straight up the road and missed the trees but it did no such thing. It flew off at right angles to the road, through dense second-growth timber and had no trouble."

Mothman, Come Back!

From 1966 through 1968, more than one hundred people in Point Pleasant, West Virginia, and the surrounding area reported seeing a giant, winged creature. They called it "the bird," but the press dubbed it "Mothman." (The Batman TV series was very popular at that time.) This critter was usually described as being taller than a big man, with blazing red eyes and a wingspan of only ten feet. Yet it was able to fly faster than a speeding car.

Significantly, some of the town's leading citizens, including a banker, the wife of a police officer, and a minister, all reported seeing essentially the same thing. Yet the creature failed to leave footprints, feces, or other physical evidence. After a flurry of sightings over a two-year period, it seemed to vanish forever. This proved once again that eyewitness testimony is of little value when you are dealing with Fortean events. A thousand people could all see the same thing at the same time and it still isn't proof that the object or entity is a real, physical, corporeal resident of our dimension. Years ago I coined the phrase, "distortions of reality" to describe occurrences such as these.

Other Mothmen or pseudo-pterodactyls have been reported since in the area around Brownsville, Texas, in England, and in South America.

Dinosaurs on the March

There is a place in Massachusetts where people have been seeing dinosaurs in recent years. (I'm not going to tell you exactly where. There's no sense starting a stampede to the spot, which is on private property anyway.) These huge animals seem to melt into nothingness in a small, wooded area. Other events in the same area suggest that some kind of time warp may exist there. Dinosaurs have an uneasy habit of reappearing every few years someplace on this planet, as I have noted in previous columns.

We have dinosaur reports from France, Italy, Switzerland, Texas, Ohio, Illinois, and many other places over the past three decades. Local police often take the sightings very seriously and turn out posses and helicopters to conduct vain searches. The dinosaurs vanish into thin air, leaving little behind but a Cheshire grin.

The truth seems to be that the human eye—and the human mind—can be tricked into perceiving almost anything. Airline pilots have reported almost as many big birds as UFOs. Bigfoot has left footprints in the dirt of almost every state. Scientists have spent large grants to penetrate Africa, where pygmies have long reported seeing dinosaurs frolicking in isolated lakes. Whatever these things may be, they are clearly a lot smarter than we are and they show themselves to us only when they feel like it.

Unfortunately, they don't seem to feel like it very often. And when they see us invading their territory loaded down with expensive cameras and tape recorders they always slip into hiding, thumbing their large noses as they go.

The Search Goes On

An old clipping from an unidentified newspaper in Pennsylvania dated March 6, 1972, forwarded by Robert Lyman, Jr., states, "...the actual evidence of the mammoth bird were pictures that appeared in many newspapers about 30 years ago." Lyman wrote not long ago, "No one can find a copy but one man reported he saw the picture only two or three months ago, but can't remember where...Hy Cranmer, who lived at Hammersley Fork, had a copy. It was burned when Cranmer's home was destroyed by fire. That photo seems to be as elusive as bird itself."

People continued to have random sightings of the big bird in Pennsylvania in the 1960s and early '70s, particularly in a region known as the Black Forest. An old-timer named Bill Burgin insists that the photo appeared in *True Western* magazine and says, "I can close my eyes and I can see the bird."

We are conducting another search through the files of the previously mentioned *Tombstone Epitaph.* If any reader out there has a file of old issues of *True Western,* perhaps he or she can flip through them. Meanwhile

I want to thank all those who have taken the time and trouble to write to me about this.

April 1991

School for Gypsies

Somewhere in the vast city of New York, on some sinister side street in a darkened slum area, there seems to be a school for gypsies. I discovered this interesting fact several years ago while doing a series of magazine articles on gypsies after an outbreak of a chain of vacant stores. Although fortunetelling parlors are expressly forbidden by New York law, gypsy storefronts appeared suddenly almost everywhere in the 1970s. Usually they were occupied by one or two exotic-looking ladies in gypsy dress who advertised that they would give you a "special reading" for only two dollars. As part of my rigorous research, I visited many of these storefronts and reluctantly parted with two bucks at each one.

My first discovery was that two dollars wouldn't get you much. For five dollars I could get my palm read and learn that I would live to be one hundred years old. For twenty-five dollars they promised to pull out all stops, gaze into their crystal balls, shuffle their Tarot cards, and solve all of my personal problems forever. At a few of the places I did cough up the twenty-five big ones and, true to their promise, they solved all kinds of problems that I never knew I had. Some of them even put their hand on my knee and subtly hinted that I was so awesomely attractive they might give me far more than twenty-five dollars' worth.

What impressed me the most, however, was the odd fact that all these ladies were handing me a carefully memorized and rehearsed line. They all delivered the same, exact speech, word for word! It seemed that they had all been trained by the same Queen of the Gypsies and had learned to be psychics by rote. From vacant store to vacant store, their patter never varied. None of them ad-libbed anything. They were using what was apparently a sure-fire routine—a "cold reading" guaranteed to work on almost everyone. They said all the things that we all want to hear. I was going to receive some unexpected wealth. I was told I would enjoy great health all my days. Gorgeous women would fling themselves at me. I had one terrific future to look forward to.

It was obvious that gypsy fortunetelling had become a franchise operation. All of these ladies had been trained in some hidden school for gypsies where they teamed to dispense hope instead of hamburgers. Then they bought into a vacant store, hung out their two dollar sign and went into business.

My next discovery was that none of them were really gypsies. They were Spaniards, Italians, Haitian—one was even a Greek. But none of them had any gypsy blood. That school was not only teaching them to tell fortunes, it was teaching them to be fake gypsies!

Fed Up!

Although I made a serious effort to locate it, I never did find the school for gypsies. Nor could I discover who was behind the whole operation. Eventually the chain of vacant stores disappeared, driven out by high rent increases, I suppose. The few fortunetelling parlors that remain seem to be operated by real gypsies, and they try to extract more from you than a mere two bucks.

No one knows exactly how many gypsies there are. They don't fill out census forms. Legend has it that they don't even use the mail or telephones. They seem to have their own communication system and they live in a strange world completely separated from the rest of us. The United Nations once estimated there are about five million gypsies in the United States. They ride around in very expensive cars and are known for their shrewd business acumen. While the men are out selling aluminum siding to suburbanites, the women are busy predicting the future in the seamier side of towns.

Actors like Robert Duvall and Cornel Wilde have made movies about gypsy life while academic "gypsiologists" put out learned newsletters of befuddled information about the movements of tribes and the elections of new gypsy kings. Recently some alleged gypsies in the Boston area received some publicity for their campaign to get the gypsy moth renamed.

Yes, the gypsies are fed up with all the anti-gypsy media slurs.

They even resent having a moth named after them.

It is a sad truth that gypsies are one of the most maligned racial groups on Earth, and certainly they are the victims of as much or more prejudice than any other ethnic group. Nobody has anything kind to say about gypsies, and they have been chased from country to country for the past five hundred years.

Back in the 1930s, Adolf Hitler and his enterprising associates thought they had the final solution to the gypsy "problem." They spread the word that Nazi scientists were undertaking a special study of the gypsies and their interesting social practices. They offered free food and housing to any gypsies who wished to participate. Gypsy camps were set up on the outskirts of several cites and, surprisingly, the usually wily and wary gypsies flocked to them. After a few days of interviews and physical exams they were all herded into trains, and the next thing they knew they were in the dreaded Nazi concentration camps.

About two million gypsies from all over western Europe were slaughtered in the gas chambers. There were very few gypsies left at the end of the war, and they were all behind the Iron Curtain in Hungary, Poland, and other eastern European nations.

Since the Communist countries were devoted to the premise that everyone should work for the state and since the gypsies had a traditional aversion for anything called "work," gypsy life in eastern Europe was very difficult. Many were reduced to living like animals in the forests, barely existing on the fringes of society. Poverty and deprivation forced them into lives of crime. They were chased and hunted throughout the eastern bloc. Anti-gypsy prejudice ran higher than ever.

The Walls Come Down

In countries such as Romania, where the gypsies are the largest minority group, their lives are nightmarish. They have the highest illiteracy rates, the shortest life expectancy, and the highest rates of infant mortality.

Suddenly, in 1989, eastern Europe shed the communist system. The Wall in Berlin came tumbling down. Millions of long-oppressed people poured across the borders. Among the first to flee were the gypsies.

Those who couldn't get out face a worse fate than ever. The leading gypsy spokesman in Romania, Nicholas Gheorghe, general secretary of the Democratic Union of Rom, recently observed, "We are the only victims of the political changes. We stand to suffer the most under the new freedoms."

Emil Scuka, a lawyer and leader of the some eighty thousand gypsies in Czechoslovakia, noted sadly that "Everyone hates the gypsies." The German news magazine *Der Spiegel* quoted Ion Cioaba, another Romanian gypsy, as saying, "My people were tormented before the revolution and are tormented after. If something doesn't change quickly, we are headed for another Holocaust. Two million Gypsies with Romanian passports will soon be standing at the German border, wanting in."

Already twelve thousand gypsies are known to have immigrated into what was West Germany. Many more are on the way, traveling from as far away as Russia. Most are in miserable health and their futures in countries that haven't even seen a gypsy in over forty-five years are uncertain. There is already a growing outcry, demanding to "send 'em back where they came from."

The trouble is, not even the gypsies know where they came from. They are a people without a country.

We can make one prediction, though. In the coming months Germany will find itself with new chains of vacant stores blossoming everywhere.

May 1991

A New Kind of Treasure

Everyone dreams of finding a valuable painting by an old master in their attic or discovering a shoebox filled with thousand-dollar bills abandoned on a park bench. This kind of thing does happen to a few lucky people every year. It happened to the Tinning family in Gore, Oklahoma, just last summer. Unfortunately, they found a treasure so rare it had no value because no one could put a price on it.

While on a picnic on August 11, 1990, JoAnn Tinning found a 1992 penny!

Tinning was wandering around with one of those electronic metal detectors—her hobby is hunting for lost coins—and she wasn't very lucky that day. She only found a couple of dimes and, just before leaving the picnic area, she detected an old wheat penny buried under about six inches of dirt. The coin had apparently been there for a long time and was quite worn. She hardly glanced at it as she tossed it into her bag. But later her son took a close look at it and realized there was something very strange about the date on it. It was stamped 1992-D.

In the weeks that followed, the Tinnings showed their penny to a variety of coin collectors and experts. All scoffed at first, before they studied it under lenses and microscopes. Although counterfeit coins of all kinds are not unusual and experts can alter the date on a coin, this wheat penny (so named because it has stalks of wheat on the obverse side) seemed to be authentic. There were no tool marks on the date or other giveaway signs of tampering. Of course, they stopped minting wheat pennies years ago and there are no plans to mint any next year, so the coin could not have somehow come from the future. Was it just a mistake like those famous stamps imprinted with upside-down airplanes? (They were worth a fortune.)

The Tinnings checked further. Since there are no 1992 coins in the catalogs, this was one of a kind and there was no way to evaluate it. Next year, it will no longer be unique. There will be plenty of 1992 coins around. "Years in the soil have taken a toll on it," Mrs. Tinning wrote in the December 1990 issue of *Lost Treasure* magazine. "Nothing recent has been done to change the date. All the wear and tear is even across the face. If it was altered, it had to have been done when the penny was new, whenever that was."

Pennies from Heaven

Coins from the future are admittedly rare but, as every Fortean knows, coins from the ancient past do have an uncanny way of turning up. In at least one memorable incident recorded by the late Ivan Sanderson, it rained not frogs and fishes but big English pennies in Ramsgate, England, in February 1969.

Sanderson, the founder of the Society for the Investigation of the Unexplained (S.I.T.U.) compiled extensive lists of things that had dropped out of the sky over the centuries. Everything from carved stone pillars to hundred-year-old newspapers have dropped unexpectedly from clear skies.

Other peculiar anomalistic debris have been found buried in the ground like the 1992 penny. Charles Fort waded through old scientific journals and newspapers to catalog thousands of these items. "We have a notion that there have been disasters aloft, and that coins have dropped here," Fort wrote in the 1920s in his classic *The Book of the Damned*, "that inhabitants of this earth found them or saw them fall, and then made the coins imitatively: It may be that coins were showered here by something of a tutelary nature that undertook to advance us from the stage of barter to the use of a medium. If coins should be identified as Roman coins, we've had so much experience with 'identifications' that we know a phantom when we see one. But, even so, how could Roman coins have got to North America—far in the interior of North America or buried under the accumulation of centuries of soil—unless they did drop from wherever the first Romans came from? Ignatius Donnelly, in *Atlantis*, gives a list of objects that have been found in mounds that are supposed to antedate all European influence in America: lathe-made articles, such as traders from somewhere would supply to savages, marks of the lathe said to be unmistakable. Said to be: of course we can't accept that anything is unmistakable."

In the 1800s, farmers' plows often turned up things in the American soil that should not have been there. Some were finely wrought vases and even crosses of silver that were apparently very, very old. "Indian mounds" yielded metallic objects, like swords and breastplates, that the early Native American people could not have made. A few of these things seemed to be not only out of place but also out of time. Scholarly archaeologists have a neat way of handling such discoveries—they ignore them.

The Ancient Battery Mystery

In 1938, there was an exception. A German archaeologist named Dr. Wilhelm Konig was digging into a hill in Iraq when he unearthed ten ancient vases that appeared to have been used as dry cell batteries thousands of years ago. Later, more of these mysterious batteries turned up in other parts of the Middle East. Author Willy Ley, the famous rocket expert, wrote extensively about these peculiar discoveries and the General Electric High Voltage Laboratory in Pittsfield, Massachusetts even made a duplicate of the ancient batteries. They worked, generating about two volts. This could explain some of the gold and silver plated objects found in very old tombs. Plating is done by an electrical process.

When I visited Baghdad in the mid-1950s, I stopped by the Baghdad Museum and asked to see the famous batteries. They didn't know what I was talking about. The museum in Berlin is also supposed to have some of the batteries, but when I was there it somehow never occurred to me to ask to see them. (Along this same line, every Fortean has heard of the Piri Riis maps, pre-Columbian maps of North and South America which Captain

Arlington Mallory found in the National Archives. Professor Charles Hapgood did a fine study and a wonderful book about them. But on one of my treks to the National Archives a few years ago I couldn't find any employee who had even heard of them and we couldn't find any trace of the maps in the assorted indices and reference catalogs. Maybe there really is a sinister conspiracy...)

According to an Associated Press report in the early 1980s, an archaeological team in China dug into a tomb more than two thousand years old and found a goodly supply of aluminum pots and pans. So what, you say?

Aluminum is not found naturally like iron or gold. It is a metal that we manufacture from bauxite by an electrical process. So the big question is: where did the ancient Chinese pot makers get their aluminum from? Did they have batteries, too?

Our Very Weird Planet

What kind of a world do we live on? A bizarre variety of debris has been raining on us since the beginning of time. People have been killed by hailstones the size of bowling balls. Big chunks of glass have come crashing out of the blue, along with a weird assortment of metal, raw meat, and even blood.

When we dig into the dirt under our feet we find many other things that shouldn't be there: Viking relics where no Viking has ever trod, metal plates engraved with symbols that nobody can translate, massive stone structures that make no sense at all. Above the ground there are old stone towers that were here before the earliest Native Americans arrived, Stonehenge-type circles are everywhere, along with pyramids (the biggest one of all is in Mexico and was apparently built thousands of years before the Egyptians thought of it), and paved highways in places where there was no use for them.

So on a quiet summer picnic in Oklahoma, a woman with a metal detector unearthed a 1992 penny in the year 1990.

Charles Fort would have liked that.

June 1991

Bumps on the Head

You've seen them in the windows of old antique shops: Placid-looking porcelain heads covered with lines and numbers. They used to sell for a couple of dollars and everyone had one on their mantle. Now they belong to the age of player pianos and iceboxes that used real ice. In the last century they were an important part of a national fad that is now almost completely forgotten.

Back in those good old days people were fondling each other's heads, feeling bumps and comparing them with the numbers on those porcelain busts. This was called phrenology, and in the 1800s phrenologists were highly esteemed scientists.

A German doctor named Franz Joseph Gall started the craze in 1796 when he decided that a person's character and mental faculties could be determined by the size and location of the bumps on the head. Later, this evolved into a system of fortunetelling. Expert bump-readers charged high fees and were consulted by businessmen and politicians. Dr. Gall, however, was run out of Vienna in 1802 and settled in Paris where he wrote a number of best-selling books and found universal acceptance for his theories. By the middle of the nineteenth century the whole world was into bump reading. Phrenologists replaced astrologers in the royal courts and common folk everywhere had their heads read on a regular basis.

No one dared to get married until a phrenologist had passed judgment on the bumps on their future spouse's head. Bad bumps would surely foretell a bad marriage.

Dr. Gall's theories were, unfortunately, not sound anatomically. The size and shape of the skull and the bumps of fat in the skin had no real bearing on the structure of the brain underneath. The fad slowly died out and all those porcelain heads ended up in old curiosity shops.

Skull Ridges and Other Wonders

A new kind of phrenology enjoyed a revival in Mexico in the 1970s. A group of highly trained, solidly credentialed medical doctors in Mexico City made what seemed to be a remarkable discovery. They had become involved in a complicated medical and psychiatric study of UFO contactees and what are now called "abductees." Mexico had more than its share of such people, and a few Mexican contactees had even attained wide fame.

During a visit to Mexico City in 1977, these doctors wined and dined me while they paraded some of their prize contactees before me and urged me to feel their heads. They had found that people who had close encounters with unidentified objects had later developed strange ridges and bumps on their heads. This seemed to be the one characteristic all the Mexican contactees had in common. The doctors knew that I had carried out extensive studies of hundreds of American contactees and isolated many common genetic and psychological factors. But I have to admit that I never felt the bumps on their heads. This was a whole new line of research.

The ridges on the Mexican heads were very pronounced, not like the small lumps and indentations that formed the basis for phrenology. But we had to ask: Could there be any unnatural anatomical explanation for this phenomenon? How could a flying saucer cause a ridge in the human cranium? This was as puzzling as the red marks that appeared below the right ear of American contactees in the 1960s. The latter would often last for weeks and were studied by Dr. Edward Condon during his UFO study at Colorado University.

In Europe, there had been an epidemic of red marks on the stomachs of UFO percipients.

By June 1967, I had concluded that we would never be able to capture an actual flying saucer, so our only hope of learning anything about the phenomenon was to perform more complete medical studies of the percipients. The medical evidence was, in fact, vast and fascinating. The Mexican doctors were aware of some of my private papers on these matters and had tried to follow my lead.

The next logical step was to x-ray the lumpy heads.

Spots on the Brain

A well-known novelist, Whitley Streiber, carried the Mexican study further when he set up an expensive research project to x-ray the brains of some percipients in the 1980s. He consulted some of the leading brain experts and x-ray technologists. They found something as remarkable as the Mexican ridges. Tiny, opaque dots appeared in the x-rays indicating that some kind of foreign object was deep inside the brains of some of the percipients!

In a speech before the New York Fortean Society on May 20, 1989, Streiber showed slides of the x-rays. The objects in the brain tissue were plainly discernible. Doctors who examined the plates were baffled.

Unfortunately, the only way to resolve the mystery is to carry out a serious brain operation and probe for the objects. This could be both very dangerous and very expensive. No one is likely to volunteer for such an operation.

Meanwhile, there is a growing cult of saucer enthusiasts who contend that the opaque dots are implants designed to control the human brain and were inserted by fiendish entities from some far-off planet. The big flaw in this notion is that our own medical technology had attained the capability for doing this back in the 1950s. We were implanting things into animals a generation ago. Some of these experiments received a considerable amount of publicity. Ferocious bulls could be turned into mild-mannered Ferdinands at the press of a switch.

By the 1980s our own studies of high frequency sound waves and electromagnetism had reached a point where any home hobbyist could build a simple device that would affect humans and animals in the same way

UFOs had been reported to affect us. Many of the things that had seemed so mysterious in the 1940s and '50s were now part of our own technological arsenal. Putting implants in brains is not at all necessary if you want to control the human and or nervous system.

Where Did It All Start?

All of this began a very long time ago, and men have been trying to interpret it for thousands of years. Today we examine mysterious marks on our legs, our stomachs, below our ears, and even in our brains, and we assume that these are all caused by mysterious lights in the sky. Back in 1484, these things were called "Devil's marks" and people who possessed them were burned at the stake. In ancient Greece, such marks were regarded as proof that the percipients had visited the gods on Mount Olympus.

A manual for professional witch hunters, the *Malleus Maleficarum*, published three centuries ago, is still in print and available from Dover Books. It is not an easy book to read but anyone willing to wade through its turgid text will suffer the shock of recognition. All of the things being reported in modern UFO cases are buried in this book in another frame of reference. At that time it was the Devil who got the blame.

As always, we seem to be traveling in circles, recovering the same old ground, generation after generation, finding new names and new explanations for very old manifestations of phenomena that have always existed on this planet and have always troubled the human race.

We can only wonder what new explanations will be in vogue five hundred years from now. Wait 'til they discover they have lumps on their heads, too!

July 1991

The Worst Kept Secret of All Time

You've been saying it all your life, never realizing that you were lying through your teeth. It ranks up there with all the great prevarications of the twentieth century such as "the check is in the mail." You may have even muttered it in the last few days. It's as common as the now-tiresome complaint, "We could put a man on the moon, how come we can't..."

It was produced by some propaganda machine deep in Washington, D.C., nearly half a century ago, and people have been repeating it ever since. Most of us still believe it. Despite all that has happened, we still like to think that the atomic bomb was the best kept secret in history.

Baloney.

The sobering truth is that the atomic bomb was probably the worst kept secret in history and today there are whole libraries attesting to this uncomfortable fact. Any high school student who wants to build an atom bomb as a class project can find complete instructions in thousands of books and magazine articles. The late Abby Hoffman once said he could foresee a day when there would be an atomic bomb in every garage. If your neighbor refused to return your lawnmower, you could nuke him.

Back in the 1930s, a whole generation grew up watching movie serials involving atom smashers, mad scientists working on atomic rays, and nuclear plans being passed from spy to spy, never suspecting that all that futuristic fiction would come true in their lifetime.

At the prompting of Albert Einstein, President Roosevelt set up the Manhattan Project early in World War II. Its goal was to build an atomic bomb. General Lesley Groves, Dr. J. Robert Oppenheimer, and a large band of nuclear scientists began the task behind a curtain of tight secrecy...or so they thought. But they had hardly begun rubbing one atom against another when, to their abject horror, a popular pulp magazine called *Astounding Science Fiction* hit the stands with a story by one Cleve Cartmill describing how to set off a nuclear explosion. His explanation was so accurate that the F.B.I. and Groves' security people flew into a paranoid frenzy. Agents frantically visited newsstands around the country, trying to buy up all copies of the magazine. It was science fiction's finest hour and the incident has become legendary.

Inside "The Thing"

In August 1945, three atomic bombs were exploded and their existence was made public. A month later, a science teacher in a high school in western New York asked a fifteen-year-old boy to explain how the nuclear bombs worked. Making sketches on the blackboard, the boy described exactly how the bombs were constructed and how radioactive materials were turned into a critical mass. Countless other boys in other schoolrooms all over the country were delivering similar talks. By September 1945, enough information had been published in the general media that any interested person could easily learn how nuclear weapons worked.

The Atomic Age was only a month old.

Newspapermen, ranging from famous war correspondents to obscure local editors, all boasted that they had known about the atomic bomb all along. They had simply chosen not to write about it. It was hard not to be aware of it. We had built two "secret" cities, Hanford, Washington, and Oak Ridge, Tennessee, employing thousands of people from drivers and contractors to plumbers and auto mechanics. All of these people were aware that something very special was under way.

In the earlier stages, the Manhattan Project had taken over a section of the Philadelphia Naval Yard because it needed a place with a lot of water and electricity to work on metallurgical experiments. Local people there were puzzled by the appearances of bearded scientists, including Einstein himself. One young seaman named Carl Allen launched the rumor of the "Philadelphia Experiment," which is still circulating in cult circles nearly half a century later.

Equally bizarre rumors were being spread around Hanford, Oak Ridge, and, later, the massive Savannah River Project in Georgia. Most implied that the U.S. was engaged on a huge rocket project similar to Germany's Peenemunde where the V-1s and V-2s had been built.

In the torrent of books that appeared following the war, many correspondents and journalists boasted of how they had known about the atomic project. Bob Considine, Mark Hellinger, Walter Winchell, and many others claimed they had been on the inside from the start. I will quote only one, John Gunther, who was as famous as Edward R. Murrow in those long-gone days. In his best-selling book *Inside U.S.A.* (1947) Gunther observed:

"The activities of this Hanford plant were secret in the extreme—naturally. The most extraordinary and sensitive precautions were taken, but nobody could altogether hide an operation of such size. Plenty of people knew that unprecedented amounts of energy were being used; few could have realized that the temperature of the entire river rose, so enormous was this amount. I began to hear tidbits of gossip from the time I reached Seattle just as in New Mexico I had heard bizarre rumors about Los Alamos. One of the most prominent men I ever met—who had absolutely no connection with the project and who had no secret information of any kind—suggested at lunch in Seattle three weeks before the first bomb was detonated, that one part of the 'thing' was being made in New Mexico, another in Washington, and that it would be assembled somewhere else. That was pretty good guessing...."

The Leak Is Sprung

When the war ended, a triumphant General Groves boasted that it would take Russia fifty years to develop an atomic bomb. Four years later, the Soviet Union exploded its first nuclear weapon.

The war was over, the Cold War was about to begin, and a totally new horror was unleashed on the American public. It was revealed that our nuclear scientists, most of whom were refugees who had fled Hitler's Europe and found refuge in the U.S.A., had formed a spy ring and had been willfully supplying communist Russia with our key atomic secrets!

The Russians had been fully informed of our nuclear progress!

In the scandals and trials that followed, sixty-five of our scientists were indicted. One had sold a major secret for a lousy three hundred bucks. Two, Julius and Ethel Rosenberg, were later executed. During the trials, it developed that we had even supplied the Soviets with a vast amount of precious uranium.

The real nightmare was to come, however. The spy trials kicked off a nationwide hysteria against the entire intellectual community and the Jewish people in particular. We entered the darkest period in recent American history—the so-called McCarthy Era of blacklists, purges and, anti-communist paranoia. This era has been the subject of countless books, articles, TV documentaries, and major movies such as the recent *Mr. Hoover and Me* and *Guilty by Suspicion,* starring Robert DeNiro as an innocent movie producer caught up in the witch hunts. Even Dr. Oppenheimer, one of the greatest minds of this century, was engulfed by this insanity and stripped of his security clearances because he had once had a romance with a girl who was allegedly a communist sympathizer.

One of the key pieces of evidence at the trial of the Rosenbergs was a rough pencil sketch they had made of how the atomic bomb works. It was almost identical to the chalk drawing made by that fifteen-year old boy back in 1945.

I know because I was that boy.

So how secret was the atomic bomb? The Russians knew all about it. John Gunther knew about it. Cleve Cartmill knew. Only one man had never heard of it in 1945. His name was Harry S Truman. After he was sworn into office following the death of Franklin Roosevelt, Secretary of War Stimson visited the new president. "Stimson told me that he wanted me to know about an immense project that was under way," Truman wrote in his memoirs. "A project looking to the development of a new explosive of almost unbelievable destructive power. That was all he felt free to say at that time, and his statement left me puzzled. It was the first bit of information that had come to me about the atomic bomb, but he gave me no details."

So Groves' attempts at secrecy had worked on the one person who should have known.

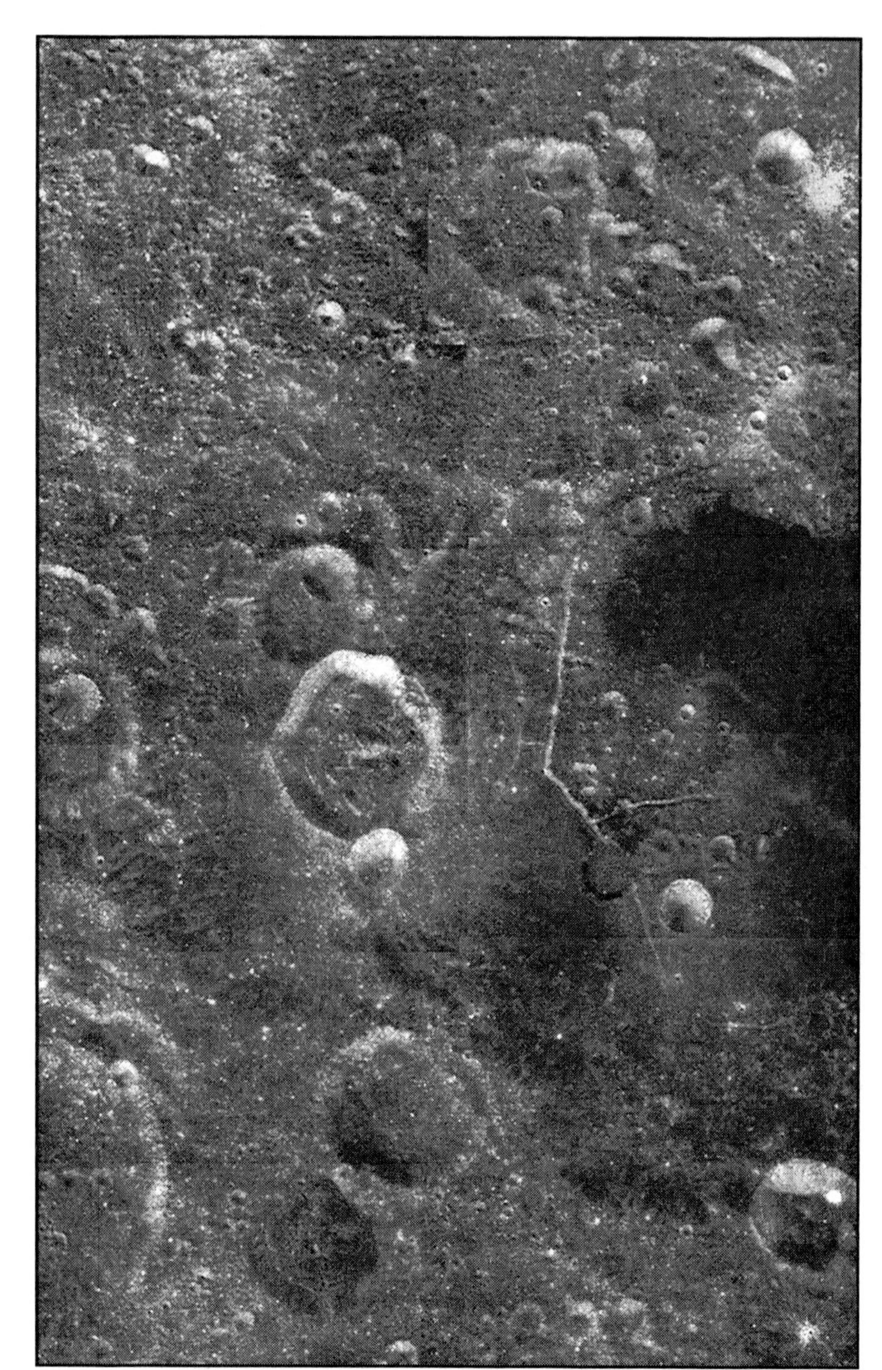

August 1991

Who Is on the Moon?

On that historic date, July 19, 1969, the Apollo 11 spaceship was orbiting the Moon, preparatory to the first lunar landing, when the astronauts received an urgent message from Mission Control in Houston, Texas. Amateur astronomers had reported seeing strange flashes of light around the crater Aristarchus. Was somebody preparing a welcome for our spacemen?

Neil Armstrong looked out the window of the command module and told Mission Control that he could see "an area that is considerably more illuminated than the surrounding area. It just has—seems to have a slight amount of fluorescence to it!"

Something was glowing on the Moon.

Again.

The Apollo crew busied themselves with the work of landing on our battered satellite and the incident was almost totally forgotten.

—But not quite.

Almost since the birth of the modern telescope, people have been seeing odd things on the Moon. In addition to the frequent inexplicable flashes of light, astronomers, both professional and amateur, have been reporting curious objects and apparent constructions such as domes, pyramids, bridges spanning craters, and big black lumps moving across the lunar landscape. Cults have sprung up based on the speculation that someone is living on our Moon.

Old Charlie Fort listed many lunar anomalies in the books he published in the 1920s and '30s. In his *Book of the Damned* he lists three pages of incidents gleaned from the scientific journals of the Victorian Age. For example, in the magazine *Popular Astronomy* he found "That upon the evening of Jan. 27, 1912, Dr. F.B. Harris saw, upon the moon, 'an intensely black object.' He estimated it to be 250 miles long and 50 miles wide. 'The object resembled a crow poised, as near as anything...I cannot but think that a very interesting and curious phenomenon happened.'"

Other reports mentioned huge, seemingly winged objects. Was our elusive Thunderbird/Mothman hiding out on the Moon? Fort planted his tongue firmly in his cheek, as he was wont to do, and suggested: "A new aspect of interplanetary inhabitancy or occupancy—worlds in hordes—or beings—winged beings perhaps wouldn't astonish me if we should end up by discovering angels—or beings in machines—argosies of celestial voyagers...."

Even the great astronomer Sir William Herschel (1738–1822) carefully noted many luminous points of light on the Moon during an eclipse.

During some periods, whole parades of lights were seen marching across the lunar face. Famed author and poet Edgar Allan Poe made a few badly needed bucks by whipping up a phony newspaper story in the 1840s about astronomers observing life forms on the Moon.

Poe's article caused a sensation for days, boosted circulation, and led to an epidemic of fake news stories about everything from sea serpents to mummy's curses.

NASA Gets into the Act

Beating the publicity drums for the approaching lunar landing in the 1960s, NASA scientists compiled and published a book of five hundred reports of things seen on the Moon. They also invented a term for them: Lunar Transient Phenomena (LTP). It was suddenly very respectable to observe thunderbirds and glowing objects fluttering about our satellite. Amateur astronomers peered through their homemade telescopes and recorded LTPs by the score. Lights were flashing all over the place. Some of the flashes persisted for a long time, thus ruling out simple explanations such as meteors crashing onto the lunar surface. One astronomer, Winifred S. Cameron, has collected over two thousand LTP reports in the last thirty years.

In some cases, the land around a crater begins to brighten and glow so that the dirt is temporarily much lighter than the dirt around nearby craters. This phenomenon has been photographed. The moon glow can become so bright that it can be seen from here on Earth.

According to *Sky and Telescope*, March 1991, "LTP sightings fall into five categories: brightenings, darkenings, reddish colorations, bluish colorations, and obscurations."

When our interest in the Moon was at its peak in the 1960s, our astronauts observed many strange anomalies. Since the lunar landings were telecast, anyone willing to sit up all night and watch their TV sets was rewarded with a variety of events, most of which were barely mentioned in the press the next day. There was no censorship per se, only neglect. So much was going on during that exciting era that we tended to forget the trivial little mysteries that plagued our spacemen… such as the eerie radio signals that sometimes interrupted the communications between the Apollo capsules and the Earth.

Orbiting astronauts also noted and photographed the Earth glow phenomenon which may be related to moon glow in some fashion. Looking down on the Earth from space, the astronauts and cosmonauts often saw glowing clouds lined up in neat rows, strange luminosities on the ground, and bright shimmering fields in the upper atmosphere. All of these things became fodder for the UFO enthusiasts, even though they are probably natural phenomena.

Searching for Answers

The most common theory for the lights on the Moon was volcanic activity and moonquakes. But our astronauts left instruments on the satellite that were supposed to measure natural seismic activity, including the impact of meteors. Readings were done over a long period via radio, of course, and the results were disappointing. Seismic activity seems to be minimal and the LTPs occur independently of such activity. In other words, the Moon doesn't necessarily light up when there's a quake.

Also, the Moon appears to be quite solid. It doesn't have a liquid core like the Earth and there is no volcanic activity. So that LTP explanation doesn't work.

A cult of civilian Moonwatchers sprang up in the 1960s and a vast literature developed. George Leonard wrote and published *Somebody Else Is on the Moon* in the mid-1970s. William L. Brian II contributed *Moongate: Suppressed Findings of the U.S. Space Program* in 1982. Brian sifted through countless NASA publications and spaceship transcripts and concluded that the public was not being told the whole truth about our discoveries in space, primarily because they involved secrets of energy and gravity.

"Consider what would happen if the United States Government issued an official announcement of these findings," Brian wrote. "A common knowledge of the nature of gravity and inexpensive ways to control it would revolutionize transportation. A new world with practically unlimited energy could emerge out of the chaos."

Lunar Madness

When the Moon isn't lighting up like a Christmas tree and the gigantic black objects aren't cruising back and forth across its surface, it is still a dynamic influence on our humble little lives. It not only controls the tides, it stimulates the sex lives of humans—and even worms. Author Paul Katzeff spent several years of his life compiling his book *Moon Madness,* a study of all the ways in which the Moon affects the denizens of this planet.

Sunspots, magnetic storms, and numerous other factors all play a role in the madness that seizes so many of us when the Moon is full. Some of the LTPs also seem to follow cyclic patterns. In other words, as Einstein tried to tell us, everything is interrelated and there may be a single cosmic law that runs the whole universe. While your dog is out baying at the full Moon and your next-door neighbor is frothing at the mouth, astronomers somewhere may be watching lights flashing on the Moon.

Some scientists have come up with lists of explanations for LTPs, covering everything from dust movements to the ever-handy piezoelectric effect. The latter occurs when rocks rub together and the ground moves, generating a strong electrical field that causes the air to glow. This phenomenon has been observed during earthquakes and some people think it can even be the cause of many UFO sightings. There isn't much evidence that it can be happening on the Moon.

For years now, members of the Association of Lunar and Planetary Observers (ALPO) have been participating in a worldwide LTP study. Files are being kept. Sightings are being recorded. Theories are being explored.

When Harrison Schmidt was circling the Moon aboard Apollo 17, he saw a flash near the Grimaldi crater. One leading theorist suggested that he really experienced a cosmic-ray flash in his eyeball.

Now there's an explanation that really makes sense.

September 1991

Demon Diggers

Someone is stealing dirt in Switzerland, and Swiss dirt owners are getting rather annoyed. According to Jan Delgado, one of the current crop of active crop circle phenomena investigators, "large holes in the earth have appeared overnight—no one witnessed their formation and none of the removed earth has ever been found and considering each hole was sequentially larger, it is a sizeable quantity."

The latest dastardly theft took place near a highway bypass outside Geneva. A hole about thirty feet in diameter and forty feet deep appeared almost magically in a farm field, directly above a highway tunnel around February 5, 1990. Geologists and tunnel engineers were baffled so the investigators consulted a German psychic named Herman Ilg. Here's his report:

"Aware of the pollution to our environment, an intelligence is monitoring its effect on life on earth.... By removing large quantities of earth, the soil can be tested for healthy or pathogenic constituents.... The method of removal is by a programmed energy beam, cutting downwards and then horizontally at 90 degrees, a pre-determined cylindrical mass of earth. Then, by a procedure involving anti-gravity, it withdraws the earth. This anti-gravitational force has a binding effect on the earth, allowing a precise and complete removal. The sampling procedure is, it is said, a way to determine the level of assistance mankind may require in the event of disaster."

Old-time Forteans will note that this is strikingly similar to the messages the UFO contactees of the 1950s used to receive.

Other holes have appeared in Echallens, Switzerland, in June 1972; Ollon, December 5, 1981, near the home of an airline pilot; and in a farm field above the village of Begnins/Vard in December 1982.

Phantom Holes in the Ground

During the worldwide epidemic of animal mutilations in the 1960s and '70s when something or someone was draining the blood from hapless domestic animals, investigators kept muttering: "Where is all that blood going?"

A variation on this cry could be applied to the hole diggers. Where is all the dirt going? The phenomena are not isolated to Switzerland. Back in the 1960s, phantom holes were springing up all over the United States and some of them appeared to be bottomless pits. That is, you could toss something into them and never hear the sound of it hitting bottom.

Sinkholes are well known. It is not uncommon for a hole to suddenly open up in a city street and swallow a few parked cars. But sinkholes are easily explained: they occur above old tunnels, underwater streams, et cetera. Our mystery holes in the ground are not sinkholes. They sometimes seem so smooth and so perfect they appear to have been dug by a large machine of some sort. The upper walls are often cut at an angle, seemingly on purpose.

In the 1950s and '60s, the phenomenon began modestly. At first the holes were only shallow depressions in the ground. Flying saucer enthusiasts regarded them as "landing sites" and a few of these cases made their way into the cultist literature as proof that flying saucers were real machines.

As time passed, the depressions were replaced by holes, which became wider and deeper and more sophisticated. I found myself standing in farm fields all over the Northeast, staring into deep holes in the ground that had appeared suddenly overnight and seemed to be deliberate excavations. The dirt from the holes was nowhere in evidence. Somebody was stealing tons of dirt without leaving tire tracks or other clues behind!

Was all this dirt being sucked into the sky somehow? Charles Fort, the leading scholar of the unknown in the 1920s, noted the existence of hundreds of reports of earthlike dirt dropping from the skies. "There are so many records of the fall of earthy matter from the sky," Fort wrote in his *The Book of the Damned* (1919) "...if I thought it necessary, I'd list one hundred and fifty instances..."

Alert Forteans still collect reports of such sky falls. Meteorologists are puzzled, however. There is no known natural force that could draw quantities of dirt upwards from one specific spot and then rain it down on another. Tornados and hurricanes are just not that selective.

Twenty years ago, when circles of pressed-down wheat were found in farm fields they were often called "saucer nests." In the 1980s, they were termed "crop circles" and the people who photographed and studied them became "cereologists." But no one ever named the holes in the ground. It would be like naming the hole in a donut. Nor did anyone ever claim to be an expert on the holes.

Nevertheless, as time passed the holes began to form complex patterns in random fields, making crosses, Xs, and weird designs. The UFO cultists tried to ignore the whole thing, just as they had ignored the animal mutilations for years. I once suggested that a master holer should be called a "concavist" but no Concavist Journal ever entered into publication.

The ultimate hole in the ground occurred at a now-forgotten alleged landing site where the hole went down a few inches, then branched out and moved in a horizontal path for a few feet. The amateur holers really got upset over that one.

As the animal mutilations increased, the farmers and the amateur holers forgot about concavism and devoted themselves to chasing imaginary vampires and blood-letting secret cults. Saucer landings and landing marks became more and more rare. Then the mutilations or "mutes" dried up and the crop circles began to dominate the 1980s.

Devilish Divots

Another very odd phenomenon took place in the 1960s. Farmers in upper New York state reported hearing loud explosions late at night, and the next morning they found huge, gaping holes in their land. Farmers in neighboring Canada were experiencing the same thing. When these sites were laid out on a map, a startling fact became clear. These holes were aligned as if some peg-legged giant had stomped across the landscape. No reasonable explanation was ever forthcoming. Perhaps some cosmic artillery had let loose a salvo on the northeastern United States.

Of course, strange explosions in the sky have been commonplace for years, particularly over Long Island and Connecticut, and are known as "skyquakes." They were occurring long before the era of the sonic boom and every couple of years they are heard in the New York City area, usually around the end of January. They don't seem to disturb the dirt.

A big dirt disturbance did take place in Okangan County, Washington, back in 1984, though. It received national publicity and perhaps you read about it in your hometown newspaper. Like most of our crop circles, it happened in a wheat field. This one was on Fred Timm's farm near the Colville Indian Reservation. There had been a small earthquake in the area on October 9, 1984. Soon afterwards, Mr. Timm discovered that a big, pear-shaped glob of his field had been somehow ripped up and moved about seventy-three feet. Then it turned about twenty degrees and settled to the ground again. The transported divot was ten feet long, seven feet wide, two feet thick and weighed tons. It had been wrenched loose, lifted into the air and moved seventy-three feet in one piece by some force we don't even know about. Perhaps it was on its way to join all that Swiss dirt when something interfered and it was dropped. (To use a Charles Fort-style citation, see *The Seattle Times*, November 23, 1984, for full details.)

Every few years some mischievous new game is launched against us and the old games are forgotten. In the 1980s, the crop circles became more and more complicated, even seeming to form symbols from ancient alphabets. Some cultists hailed it as a communication from the sky people. But I suspect a correct translation would be: HA! HA!

The holes in the ground may just be yet another game as meaningless as all the rest.

October 1991

Magic Words

In the early days of television the networks had a long list of forbidden words compiled by the mysterious Office of Standards and Practices—a fancy term for Censorship Office. These departments still exist and still try to chop out cuss words and derogatory remarks about important advertisers. Fortunately, the weird sex perverts and religious nuts who ran it in the 1950s and early 1960s are long gone.

Back in those days you could not say "pregnant" on TV. The accepted term was "in a family way." "God" was strictly forbidden. You had to say "Supreme Being." Belly buttons were absolutely taboo. If a girl appeared in a skimpy bikini, her belly button had to be carefully covered. Some fruitcake at Standards and Practices was apparently turned into a drooling zombie by the sight of a navel and assumed everyone else would react the same way.

Snakes, spiders, and most creepy-crawlie things were the network hit list. Also high on the list were "emotional" subjects. The word "crazy" was actually banned because some executive genius thought there were people out there who would go completely bonkers when they heard it. He assumed that they would froth at the mouth and scream, "Crazy! I'm not crazy!" and shove their foot through their TV screen.

Astrology was in the same category. Too many people were too emotional about astrological matters, according to network reasoning. So for many years no astrologer was seen on the tube. Another big no-no was the term "flying saucers." The Air Force didn't censor it. The network biggies did because, based on their study of their mail, flying saucers attracted dingbats, lunatics, and fugitives from the funny farm.

UFO No-Nos

Remember, that was the age of the contactees when literally thousands of people were claiming to have chatted with tall, stately, long-haired Venusians and gone for rides in their wonderful space ships.

Thousands more believed their testimony and were convinced that our little planet was a tourist attraction for extraterrestrial beings. The emotional state of these believers was a cause for concern in many quarters, not just the networks.

Gradually these network prejudices fell away. The sexual revolution took place (we lost) and Dr. Ruth was able to use words formerly confined to football locker rooms. Being crazy became part of the American way of life. Presidents consulted astrologers and other star-gazers were allowed to advertise freely on the boob tube. The flying saucer subculture was absorbed into our music and pop culture scene. Contactees and abductees were welcome guests on all the talk shows.

A twenty-foot boa constrictor, captured in Florida, appeared on the Johnny Carson show...and got rave reviews. Magicians Penn and Teller produced hundreds of oversized cockroaches for David Letterman's vast, grossed-out audience.

Close-ups of belly buttons appeared on every channel.

The Revolution of the Convoluted

Hundreds of new words were introduced in the 1960s, and lexicographers worked overtime to define them and fit them into the English language. Meanwhile, the folks at Standards and Practices labored to decide which of the new words and titles had obscene meanings. There were beatniks, hippies, yuppies, and all the meandering, monosyllabic terms of the drug culture. We no longer got robbed. We "ripped off." The Abominable Snowman was popular in the 1950s, but now he was almost replaced by Bigfoot.

New Age Neologisms

A whole generation of New Age cultists created a new slang of neologisms or made-up words, some of which gradually worked their way into general usage. Absurdities like "mother ship" and "scout ship" were part of the vernacular of the flying saucer buffs, mocked by comic strips and situation comedies. In my struggle to restore some order to the unending chaos, I tried to get the buffs to use more acceptable terms such as "percipient" for "contactee." Oddly, my campaign had a lasting effect throughout the world and "percipient" is now in wide use everywhere except in the U.S. Percipient is also a valid word for "abductee" since the UFO abduction experience is usually an altered-state condition, not a physical event. That is, it is more dreamlike than real, more a perception of the mind than an actual sensory experience.

UAPs

Early on, the U.S. Air Force realized they had a cosmic tiger by the tail and they tried to replace "flying saucer" with a number of other terms. Throughout the 1950s they advocated the use of "unidentified aerial phenomena" or UAP. Civilian hobbyist organizations did try to oblige and the two dominant groups of that era called themselves the Aerial Phenomena Research Organization (APRO) and the National Investigation Committees on Aerial Phenomena (NICAP).

But UAP was clumsy and dumb. Another term slowly moved to the forefront—Unidentified Flying Objects (UFOs)—despite the fact that the endless reports and descriptions were usually of objects that did not and could not actually fly. Technically, they were not supported by air like the wings of birds and planes. Nor did they have any visible means of propulsion in most cases. It could be said that they levitated. However, Unidentified Levitating Objects (ULOs) seemed even sillier.

It was an etymological problem of the highest order. Since many saucer buffs were cultural illiterates, there was no attempt to deal with it and UFOs became the most popular term, both in the hobbyist press and the mainstream media. The USAF's UAPs quickly became forgotten.

Fighting Our "Foes"

Unfortunately, UFO was usually pronounced "you-foe" and the word had an unpleasant, negative connotation, which left a subliminal bad taste. The more the term was used, the more negative it became in the minds of most people. This is why Madison Avenue publishers shun it and you rarely see it on the cover of a contemporary flying saucer book. Certain words are recognized as disastrous in book titles. Words such as "Philosophy" and "Devil" usually assure few sales or no sales at all. "UFO" is part of that list. Most major magazines also avoid using it on their covers. This is not censorship. It is purely a commercial consideration. If the big percipient seller of the 1980s, *Communion*, had been titled *Communion With UFOs*, it would not have sold many copies.

Another blockbuster, *Light Years*, would have laid a real egg with a UFO title. Ditto for *Intruders, Confrontation,* et cetera. The networks have relaxed their ban on UFOs and flying saucers today but a similar, more practical ban exists among the book cover designers. I may write a book titled *The Passionate Percipient* to get around the ban.

The Battle between Tellurions and Terrestrials

Many thousands of people in U.S. are CIA watchers. They publish newsletters and write books, blaming the CIA for almost everything rotten that happens. They do not refer to themselves as CIAologists, however. They are smart enough to know better. Yet, the UFO buffs proudly proclaim themselves to be ufologists—a non-word.

An impossible word. If one is really necessary, it would have to be UFO-phile.

A science fiction editor named Stefan Santesson is generally credited with coining the term "ufologist" and his pal, zoologist Ivan Sanderson, made it popular in the 1960s. It was first introduced as satirical or mocking. In fact, it was once downright insulting to be called a "ufologist." But by the end of the '60s, the term was in wide usage and every fourteen-year-old boy with an APRO membership card was calling himself an ufologist.

No Ufologists?

The sober fact is that there is no such thing and never will be. They are all UFO-philes. Before there can be ufologists, you must be able to define the necessary qualifications to be one. Since the true nature of UFOs is unknown, no one can set the criteria for the study of the objects. Those who study angels and angel reports (and this is a large if little-publicized field) call themselves aretologists. It takes a Ph.D. and extensive religious background to be an aretologist. But what does it take to be a ufologist? What field of study can prepare you for it?

There was once a scholarly debate on the words tellurian and terrestrial. Ultimately, the sci-fi writers accepted tellurian and most branches of science stuck to terrestrial. The word "ultraterrestrial" has been in the major dictionaries for generations and I introduced it to the UFO-philes in the 1960s. Many years later, the late Dr. J. Allen Hynek tried to make up a word—a neologism—for ultraterrestrial. Since his mastery of the English language was, shall we say, rather sparse, he came up with meta-terrestrial. This was complete misusage. Metaphysical started out as a neologism and is now accepted, but meta-terrestrial will never make it as a real word. And since ultraterrestrial has always existed as a perfectly legitimate term, there is no need for meta-terrestrial.

As you may have guessed, I once worked as an editor on the Funk & Wagnalls dictionary. I have sat through many dreary conferences trying to decide if some new word is really a word at all. I have seen many neologisms work their way into the language, starting back in the 1940s when Richard Shaver introduced many of the terms that are still being used by the UFO-philes today. His "deros" became the "greys" of the modern UFO lore and forty years from now people will still be inventing new words to replace old neologisms.

November 1991 (FATE's 500th issue)

"I Remember Lemuria, Too"

I was riding in a rickshaw in Calcutta, India, when I read my very first issue of *Mad* magazine. It somehow seemed entirely correct—a perfect time and place for the occasion. Totally incongruous. An overeager young Indian man was trotting in front of me. He was proudly hauling me through the Calcutta marketplace while I studied that fascinating new piece of Americana.

My first encounter with FATE magazine several years earlier was not quite so colorful. I bought it at newsstand next to the old Third Avenue "El" in New York City, and I probably had to step over a few drunken bums on the sidewalk as I made my way back to the newspaper office where I worked.

I had been surprised to find some issues of *Mad* in the stall of a street vendor in Calcutta, but FATE was no surprise. I knew it was coming and I looked forward to it. At the ripe old age of eighteen I was already a closet Fortean and frequently got into arguments with my cynical journalist friends about "flying disks" and sea serpents.

The appearance of FATE promised to vindicate me.

Ray Palmer and the Shaver Mystery

Ray Palmer, co-founder of FATE with Curtis Fuller, had been a part of my life since 1944 when I began reading *Amazing Stories,* the science fiction magazine that he then edited. I didn't realize then that he would be a continuing part of my life until his death in 1977.

Three weeks after Kenneth Arnold reported seeing nine "flying saucers" (an event that was almost completely ignored by the general news media in the Northeast), I hitchhiked four hundred miles to New York City, arriving with seventy-five cents and a cardboard suitcase filled with manuscripts. It was 1947 and I was seventeen years old. New York was so safe that on steamy hot summer nights people often left their apartments with a pillow and slept in Central Park! Only movie theaters were "air cooled" in those days.

I quickly became the editor of a literary quarterly called *Poets of America* and I soon knew every poet, writer, editor, and artist in the vast cultural community that was Greenwich Village. Later I became a feature writer on *Limelight*, a weekly tabloid devoted to entertainment news. I also started writing for television, then in its infancy, at station WABD and what would become the Dumont Network.

All the while I continued to read "sci-fi." There were about two hundred different pulp magazines on the market in the 1940s. These sold mostly for a dime and covered a wide range of subjects—from the Wild West, hard-boiled detectives, and mysterious characters like the Shadow and Fu Manchu to World War I flying stories (a chap named Donald Keyhoe was a frequent contributor to those) and erotic love tales. They were printed on the cheapest paper available—a rough, unfinished substance called, of course, pulp.

Literally thousands of writers (who were paid a penny a word), artists, and editors earned a meager living from those pulp magazines. Ray Palmer was one of those. He worked for the vast Ziff-Davis pulp empire in Chicago.

I followed the birth and growth of the Shaver Mystery in the pages of *Amazing Stories*, more astonished than enthralled. Richard Shaver was an aspiring writer who allegedly had spent time in prison and was also allegedly ensconced, rather frequently, in mental hospitals for bouts with schizophrenia. He allegedly admitted to having been influenced by a 1919 novel called *The Moonpool* by A. A. Merritt.

In this book Merritt had introduced such concepts as circular aircraft and demonic little grey men with features now familiar in the modern abduction lore. Shaver made a few slight modifications and updated *The Moonpool* in a series of badly done stories beginning with "I Remember Lemuria."

Palmer rewrote the stories and the Shaver Mystery, as it was soon called, was launched. Essentially, the stories claimed that the world was being controlled by Detrimental Robots—DeRos—who lived in underground hideaways.

As a serious sci-fi fan (I published a "fanzine" titled *Lunarite*), I was dismayed by the overall quality of *Amazing Stories.* The flying disks, crashed spaceships, and little grey "deros" that filled its pre-1947 pages annoyed all of us, but a certain segment of the public was drawn to them like a magnet. Palmer was flooded with letters from people who claimed experiences with these things. Circulation jumped.

The average sci-fi 'zine sold about twenty-five thousand copies in those days, but suddenly, stacks of *Amazing Stories* were appearing in the racks and each issue was selling out! Palmer had found a winner in Shaver and knew how to exploit him. Shaver became a literary star. In the mid-1940s he even began publishing his own *Shaver Mystery Magazine* for fifty cents a copy—a then-unheard-of sum. Some national magazines, such as *Liberty,* sold for a mere nickel. Only the weighty magazines *Esquire* and *Fortune* dared charge half a buck.

Roots of Weirdness

A psychic named Mark Probert began to contact "space people" in 1945 by a process now known as "channeling." Dr. Mead Layne, a West Coast psychical researcher, also began studying flying disks around the same time. Tiffany Thayer's Fortean Society was on an outer space alert, too, while *Amazing Stories*' growing readership mobilized behind Shaver. By 1947, thanks in large part to these busy groups, there was a sizable flying saucer subculture in the United States. They were not at all surprised when Kenneth Amold's sighting made headlines in the western states that year. So contrary to the modern story, 1947 was not the beginning of the modern UFO era. Folklorists and historians can say that Merritt began it in 1919 and then it exploded in 1944 with the appearance of the "foo fighters" in

Europe and the introduction of the Shaver Mystery in the U.S. By 1947, thousands of people were eagerly watching the skies. When I compiled an article on the pre-Arnold sightings reported by the press in 1947, even I was astonished by how many there were. (The article appeared in a special 1967 anniversary issue of Jim Moseley's UFO-oriented magazine *Saucer News.*)

I followed *Amazing Stories* and Palmer's career with fascination, perhaps being more interested in it all because of the sociological and psychological implications—main concerns of mine even then. Something very odd and potentially very important was happening, but I couldn't quite untangle it. I had no idea that we would still be writing about the subject of UFOs nearly half a century later.

In 1947, major magazines and newspapers began to deal with Forteana. Even such unlikely sources as *Variety*, the "bible" of show business, began to carry saucer reports. There were all kinds of rumors, many of which are still being repeated today. For example, the big rumor of 1947 and '48 was that the federal government was about to issue a sensational statement about the subject. Other rumors said that the public was being prepared through the news media and films. (Cheap, grade-Z movies on UFOs began to appear in 1948, culminating in the superb *The Day the Earth Stood Still* in 1952. That film became the classic by which all UFO movies are measured. Some of the modern UFO lore seems to have been built around it.) Both of these rumors were still being circulated in 1990.

Palmer was abruptly fired as editor of *Amazing Stories* and the magazine abruptly dropped the very profitable Shaver Mystery. Palmer later claimed that he was the victim of a sinister conspiracy.

Actually, most of the pulp magazines were already doomed by postwar inflation and that newfangled thing called television. In a single month, November 1941, the pulp publishers all threw in the towel simultaneously. Hundreds of magazines went out of business. A few of the sci-fi pulps managed to hold on, however, including *Amazing Stories.* But it was never the same after Palmer's departure.

Hints of Conspiracy

Then as now, the sci-fi fans were better educated, more culturally literate, and better organized than any of the other hobby groups. They followed the saucer/Shaver/Palmer situation very closely, and knew almost instantly that Palmer was planning to publish a new magazine on his own. The war had created a big market for digest-sized magazines, and there were over twenty different ones on the newsstands in the 1940s. Magazine distributors even preferred the format. It was therefore entirely logical that Palmer's new offering would be a digest of some sort.

Forteana In New York

New York City had a very lively Fortean community in those days.

Charles Roberts ran a basement bookstore that stocked rare books on Atlantis, Nostradamus, and Fort. It was a gathering place for all kinds of eccentric authors and students of the unknown. You could buy a good used book in mint condition for a dime. Although Roberts is long gone, his book on Nostradamus is still in print.

Stewart Robb, who promoted the notion that Sir Francis Bacon was the real author of all of Shakespeare's plays, conducted weekly séances in his Hotel Wentworth suite and was surrounded by all the Forteans of the day. Everyone from famed playwright William Saroyan and a very young Marlon Brando to Loker Raley and Paris Flammonde could be found in Robb's suite. Nita Naldi, a silent film star, was a regular, along with a long list of newspapermen and characters like "Prince" Robert Rohan DeCourtnay, Joe Gould ("Professor Seagull"), Maxwell Bodenheim, Ben Hecht (the great screenwriter), Elmo Russ (who wrote some of the worst songs I've ever heard), and Ben Benson, "the king of the hoboes."

Ivan T. Sanderson was busy with radio broadcasts, as was Walter McGraw. Every Sunday a man named Nelson Olmstead gave a Fortean talk on a radio network and, of course, Robert Ripley of Believe It or Not fame was always close by, throwing parties on his Chinese junk in the harbor. "Sabu, the elephant boy," a very popular movie star, also stopped by whenever he was in New York from the West Coast. He had grown up in Brooklyn.

Numerous restaurants and cafeterias also hosted Fortean gatherings, and talk of flying disks was reverberating from their walls long before Arnold reported his sighting. The familiar argument that "there must be millions and millions of inhabited planets out there" was already a bore in 1947.

A network of automats across the city was open twenty-four hours a day. Swarms of Forteans hovered in those on 57th Street and 14th Street. Shabby, middle-aged men carrying bags of books and newspapers collected in Union Square and Columbus Circle (both then havens for soapbox speakers), to argue about everything from obscure political concepts to Howard Hughes's latest escapades. Hughes was a kind of Fortean hero. He was even nuttier than we were—and much richer.

In the Village, Frank MacCrudden presided over the Druid Society where skyclad young ladies danced among canvas trees salvaged from an old stage set. Frank also ran the famed Raven Poetry Society, which held an annual outdoor poetry exhibit on a fence on the edge of Washington Square. Anton Romatka, another Fortean, ran an open forum every Saturday night. After his death I was somehow elected to run the forum and did so for about two years.

There were ten major daily newspapers in New York at that time (now there are three), all filled with human interest stories and juicy Fortean reports about frog falls in Singapore and sea serpents in Zanzibar. The most important Fortean-style publication was *The American Weekly,* a Sunday newspaper supplement that I read avidly from childhood on. A. A. Merritt was the editor and he filled each issue with articles about ghosts, vampires, sky falls, pyramid lore, and, of course, unidentified flying whatzits. He also revived a 1904 newspaper article from the *Philadelphia Enquirer* (he had worked on the *Enquirer* in the early part of the century) that became the basis for the lore on the Philadelphia Experiment and the Bermuda Triangle stories. After his death in 1943, the supplement continued his editorial policies.

The bulletin board above my desk at *Limelight* was always crowded with current Fortean clippings, including the notorious "crashed saucer" headline from the Roswell paper. Whenever a big Fortean story broke anywhere I would contact the local newspaper and have them send me copies. Often I would talk to the editors and reporters on the phone. I was soon the best-informed Fortean in New York.

For a teenage boy enamored with Fortean matters and with writing aspirations, this was pure Valhalla.

Big Fight on 14th Street

No one was quite prepared for the impact of the first issue of FATE, however. Perhaps we all expected more Shaver Mystery material. Instead, it was a digest-sized blockbuster featuring Kenneth Arnold's detailed description of all the strange events surrounding Maury Island, Washington, in the summer of 1947. Time would prove it to be the most important single UFO-related case of modern times, even though the puzzle would not be unraveled for twenty years, when the AEC finally released enough information about those early days of atomic development so that the whole mystery made sense at last. It is impossible to summarize the complete Maury Island affair here. Fortunately, Arnold was a very astute observer and he was able to record every minute detail, even when those details didn't seem to make much sense at the time.

The case seemed to have everything: physical evidence, Men in Black, terrified witnesses, and, regrettably, the tragic deaths of two investigating Air Force officers and a local newspaperman. A shower of slag-like material had fallen on a boat containing one Harold Dahl and his sixteen-year-old son. One piece of slag killed the boy's dog outright and another piece injured his arm so badly that he had to be rushed to a hospital. Kenneth Arnold later obtained a large quantity of the slag and shipped some of it to

Palmer in Chicago. Palmer had a lab analyze the slag chemically and published the results. It was high in calcium and contained some other oddities. Meanwhile, Dahl's son vanished, scaring Dahl into total silence.

A generation later, long-suppressed FBI documents disclosed that the missing boy had been located in tiny Lusk, Wyoming, hundreds of miles from Tacoma. He was suffering from amnesia. The slag proved to be a waste product of the gaseous diffusion process then in use at the atomic installation in Hanford, Washington. Tons of this stuff built up constantly in the miles of pure nickel pipes in the world's biggest factory building. Disposing of all this waste was a big headache then and remains so today. Nuclear waste has always been a great controversy.

In those early days of the nuclear age, the slag and other materials were being dumped unceremoniously into the Pacific Ocean. Some of it was just buried in the ground. Kenneth Arnold had unwittingly blundered into a hot bed of spies, spy chasers, and secretive waste disposers. I spent years piecing together the whole story and corresponded extensively with Fred Lee Crisman, one of the major witnesses and a fascinating man who was working for the Veterans' Administration in 1947 but was angling for a job at Hanford. He later worked as a schoolteacher for several years and then became a well-known radio personality under the name "Jon Gold" prior to his death from natural causes in the early 1980s. I wanted to do a book on the whole Maury Island story but no publisher was interested. Eventually my rather terse book outline was published in the book *UFOs—1947–1987*, published in England by the *Fortean Times*.

The basic problem with my book is that you must be very familiar with every word of *The Coming of the Saucers* by Kenneth Arnold and Ray Palmer (Amherst Press, 1952) before my book makes any intelligible sense. It also helps if you have a working knowledge of nuclear physics and the history of the 1940s and '50s. In other words, as several editors pointed out to me, there are only a handful of people capable of dealing with it—or even caring about it.

Within weeks after the first wonderful FATE had hit the newsstands, the world's first flying saucer convention was held in the old Labor Temple on New York's 14th Street. I attended, and my only memory of it now is that there were about thirty people there, most of whom were clutching copies of FATE and shouting at each other about governmental conspiracies and the terrifying invasion from outer space.

Arnold's Maury Island account set in motion all of the basic tenets of modern ufology. The conspiracy theory hounds, the outer-space fans, the anti-Air Force and anti-government groups, and the Shaverites all found plenty in the report to turn into myth. For its part, the Air Force denounced it as a hoax—which it was. By that I mean it had no connection, really, with the flying saucers. Fred Crisman, I believe, had lied about a saucer dumping the slag, thinking he was protecting Hanford from unfavorable publicity. But he just opened a much bigger can of worms.

Another 500, Anyone?

Palmer displayed a fascinating grasp of the overall Fortean situation in the early issues by publishing articles on amnesia, missing time, Men in Black, mutilations, and other matters that still bewilder us. His early editorials, under the byline of "Robert Webster," were often worth the price of admission alone. Over the years there have been many imitators of FATE. One, *Exploring the Unknown,* was edited by the aforementioned Stewart Robb. Ultimately, only FATE survived.

A Doorway to the Unknown

Back in 1947, I never even suspected that one day I would write for FATE. Nor did I even dare think that I would be the one who would finally "solve" the Maury Island mess. There is no question that the early period—1944 to 1952—was the most exciting phase when we were all so young and suddenly discovering a vast world of the unknown, complicated beyond anything we could imagine. FATE magazine served as the doorway to that world.

It is still introducing newcomers to all the strangeness that is out there. And the sci-fi fans are still trying to ignore it all.

December 1991

Burn Before Reading

Everyone who has served in the military in the past fifty years has been baffled by the fact that official toilet paper rolls always come in a crushed condition. Some sinister force has been squeezing our Charmin! The truth about this evil plot is that back in World War II some genius figured out that we could get more rolls of toilet paper into a carton if we crushed them first. Since shipping space is always a problem, lopsided tissue rolls have been standard ever since.

The military and the bureaucracy love solutions like flattened paper rolls. So much so that in Washington, D.C., there are annual award dinners to hand out prizes to "faceless bureaucrats" who have found new ways to use paper clips or save a few bucks by recycling bubble gum wrappers.

When I was working as a consultant inside the bureaucracy in the 1970s, there were whole offices filled with people who were devoted to the "consumer problems" of other bureaucrats. In fact, more people seemed to be employed to service the bureaucracy than to help those pitiful wretches known as taxpayers. They were far more concerned with government lunch rooms and car pools than with impoverished slums, inflation, and urban crises.

Crushed toilet paper was one of the few things they could be proud of.

Shrinking Paper for Fun and Profit

Another wartime genius who probably received an award at a big dinner was the guy who figured out that the U.S. government could save many tons of paper by using sheets reduced from the standard 8-1/2" x 11" to 8" x 10".

Considering how much paper the government gobbles up, he was probably right.

If you have any federal forms or letters from federal agencies (and I must stress the word federal) lying around, measure them and you will find that most of them are 8" x 10". Even most of the standard IRS tax forms are 8" x 10". Virtually every memo and report that comes from the FBI, the Pentagon, and even the White House is on 8" x 10" sheets. If you have been collecting official documents as part of your interest in Fortean matters, you probably have drawers filled with 8" x 10" sheets. If you have been collecting second-generation or tenth-generation xeroxes of such documents they may be on 8-1/2" x 11" sheets, but when you measure the text you will find it was typed to fit the 8" x 10" format.

I once had to prepare a three-hundred-page briefing document for President Nixon (I worked for Elliot Richardson, a cabinet member) and I found that, after a lifetime of writing on 8-1/2" x 11" sheets, using 8" x 10" paper was like trying to write on the head of a pin. (Copies of my briefing document are still available but they are expensive to Xerox and ship. And it is terribly boring.)

Nearly everyone is aware of this 8" x 10" fact, just as nearly everyone has, at some time or another, tried to force a government form into the return envelope that came with it. Some other genius deep in some Washington catacomb figured out that the government should always send out the wrong sized envelopes with its forms!

Faking It

The only people unaware of the 8" x 10" fact seem to be those flying saucer aficionados who have always devoured pathetically obvious fake "documents." In the early days, back in the 1940s, the clever and sophisticated science fiction buffs delighted in planting phony flying saucer stories and nonsensical "documents" about little men and crashed saucers in the newsletters and hobbyzines of the day. Some of these even worked their way into the

UFO literature and are still being repeated in current books and publications.

There was so much of this hoaxing that the venerable weekly, *Life* magazine, commented on it in their May 21, 1951, issue. Fifteen years later, hoax documents were still turning up in the offices of New York magazines, but they were usually easy to detect because of the size and kind of paper used, the contents, and the style. (The hoaxers didn't know how to write bureaucratese and they didn't know the proper codes, prefixes, et cetera.) Also, nearly every government typewriter in use prior to 1960 had a special characteristic that made it simple to tell if a document had been typed on one. Early electric typewriters were expensive, huge, heavy, and costly to maintain so they didn't come into wide usage in the government until the late 1950s.

Fortunately, very few of the '60s hoaxes were published outside of the UFO newsletters and the supermarket tabloids. In a 1969 article I even wrote a terse warning about such things.

In the basement of almost every federal building in Washington and elsewhere there is usually a large supply room that is like a candy store to white collar thieves. If you have a proper government ID card you can stock up on everything from reams of 8" x 10" paper to handsome leather briefcases. Here you will also find a plethora of rubber stamps that say, "TOP SECRET," "CONFIDENTIAL," "RESTRICTED," et cetera. The most interesting thing about these stamps is that they are identical to the kind of stamps that you can buy in any large stationery store. Fortunately, the hoaxers didn't know this—until this article—and they usually manufactured their own rubber stamps that didn't even remotely resemble the real thing.

Dealing with Frauds

Remember, too, that a Xerox copy is not a "document." It is too easy to tamper with Xeroxes. That's why such copies are not admissible in a court of law (unless the source can be proven) or in journalism generally.

The 1980s proved to be the biggest decade in UFO history for fraudulent documents, photos, and fakes and hoaxes of all kinds. Sadly, the UFO-philes had not learned their lessons in the 1940s or '60s and a whole new lore grew up around the blatant fakes.

If you come across something that you suspect might be a fraud, have it checked out by one of the many bureaucratic "watch dog" groups in Washington (Ralph Nader's is the best known, but there are many others). Or ask your local senator or representative. He or she has a large staff who will help you. Writing to the agency that is allegedly the source of the fake is usually a waste of time and will produce nothing but a "brush off" letter. The hoaxers count on that.

There are many, many books available that can inform you on the workings of the government, how to locate government publications (are you on the mailing list of the Government Printing Office?), and how to check codes. Look for *Find It Fast* by Robert Berkman (a recent bestseller), The *Writer's Legal Companion* by Brad Bunnin and Peter Beren, *Latest Intelligence* by James E. Tunnell, and if you are in need of a chuckle look for the oldie but goodie *Arsenic and Red Tape* by Edmund G. Love.

If you don't want to take the time to visit a library, at least buy a ruler.

January 1992

This Is Where I Came In

"What's going to happen next?" That's the question most often asked by people who have been following weird events for years. Strange cycles are followed by the forces that distort our reality and have us running around in circles looking for sea serpents, UFOs, and giant hailstones. Just when we think we have found a significant pattern and are about to solve a baffling mystery, everything changes and we are off on another wild goose chase. The phenomena always stay one step ahead of us.

We have gone through many cycles in the past forty years and a few of us have even learned something about the real nature of the unreal. It is doubtful that we will ever make any real gains, however. We can only second-guess the enigmatic system that controls these events. We will certainly face many surprises in the 1990s.

Here are some learned predictions of coming events. They are based upon analyses of the often silly little cosmic games played out in the recent past.

An Invasion of the Monsters

Every few years we have a new monster wave that grips the attention of the press and public. Remember Momo, Lizardman, and old Three Toes? They were terrific monsters but now they're has-beens. I predict that a new monster will pop up in the next two to five years that will really make them look like sissies.

We are about due for a new dinosaur wave. Some kind of gigantic saurian is going to appear in a remote area, gobble up a few cows, and scare the daylights out of a lot of people. Local police will form posses and helicopters will search the area in vain. Television anchors will rush to the spot and sit sheepishly in some swamp waiting for the critter to reappear. UFO buffs will also flock there and make sober pronouncements about dinosaurs from outer space. All of this could take place somewhere in the South, possibly in Georgia or Louisiana.

Not Out of Gas

Back in the early 1930s there was an epidemic of automobile stallings. Long lines of cars on busy highways would mysteriously stall simultaneously and create colossal traffic jams. In Germany they tried to blame it on experimental television stations. In Italy the great Marconi was accused of tampering with radio frequencies that could stall ignition systems. In the U.S. the usual "experts" (who are these meatballs?) announced that sunspots were the cause.

We now know what really causes some of these stallings. The electromagnetic pulse (EMP) of a nuclear blast can produce the effect. The widespread power failures and communication failures of the 1960s were caused by the EMP from atmospheric bomb tests, particularly those in China. By the late 1960s, Ma Bell had spent millions taking down the telephone poles that dotted the countryside and burying all the telephone lines underground to counter the problem. They also developed "tempest shielding," a way of insulating sensitive equipment from EMP.

U.S. military forces, with their usual keen grasp of the situation, dealt with the threat of EMP by equipping all of our tanks, ships, and planes with transistorized computers and communications. Transistors are particularly susceptible to EMP and a blast two hundred miles away can cause them to malfunction. The Soviets, on the other hand, were also aware of the problem and continued to use old-fashioned radio tubes in their equipment because tubes are less vulnerable to EMP.

Modern automobiles are now loaded with transistors and are likely to be affected by EMP more than ever. Stories of mysterious stallings are already trickling in. I predict that in the near future wholesale stallings will begin to occur. They will not be caused by nuclear blasts, though. They will be caused by the much-publicized breakdown of the ozone layer and natural bombardments of cosmic rays and energy from the sun.

Mars or Bust

On the negative side, here's a prediction about space travel. You've been hearing a great deal about a planned manned space shot to the planet Mars. The idea is to send six people—three men and three women—to Mars within the next thirty years. I have followed space developments closely all my life, and wrote many articles about NASA, Dr. Goddard (the rocket pioneer), and the like back in the early 1960s. At one point I was even scheduled to take the basic astronaut training to collect material for a piece for *True* magazine. It didn't work out so I let Neil Armstrong go in my place.

Seeing Earth men and women on Mars has been a dream of mine…of all of us…since Buck Rogers and Flash Gordon started zooming around the universe. But now I regret that I must predict that it will never happen. The problems seem insurmountable. The design and construction of a Mars ship will be too costly. Our economic and political problems are just too overwhelming.

Remember, President Nixon slashed the space program to pieces back in the early 1970s, putting many scientists and engineers out of work permanently. We have just been using up the hardware that was ordered during the Kennedy and Johnson administrations. The Soviets are now way ahead of us in space, and several other countries are there as well. (Did you know that the Japanese have a satellite orbiting the Moon?) Space travel once again seems like a far-fetched dream. We'll keep sending up satellites and maybe a space station or two, but it may be centuries before humans return to the Moon or venture further out to Mars and beyond.

"Hi, Uncle Charlie. What's it like Being Dead?"

It has often been observed that all electronic equipment is prone to interference by the invisible forces that surround us. Telephones, tape recorders, television sets, and even computers can become "haunted." The literature on ghosts, UFOs, and the occult is filled with accounts of this mysterious interference. The evidence is so vast that it is safe to conclude that electrical energy can be—and often is—manipulated to support various belief systems and frames of reference. Images of deceased persons have appeared on television sets in Europe. Voices claiming to come from distant planets have been picked up on radios.

As our dependence on electronic gadgets increases, so does this interference. Experimenters scattered around the world are learning to communicate directly with these forces—forces that previously had to rely on persons with rare psychic abilities.

I predict that we are about to enter an age when anyone, anywhere (with the proper electronic gear), can communicate at will with forces or entities beyond the range of our limited human perceptions. This could happen in less than ten years. This could be a far more important breakthrough than a mere trip to Mars!

These forces cannot seem to deal with solid matter in our material world but they—or It—can juggle electrons.

There is a warning connected with this, though. Aeons of spirit mediums, wizards, witches, and psychics have learned that there is a very mischievous energy at work here. It plays games with us, tells terrible lies, and creates fearful but meaningless apparitions. Many of our most cherished beliefs are based on these games and those lies. Now that a magic door is being opened electronically between our two worlds we must proceed with great caution. In the past we learned we could not trust our own senses. Now we must learn we can't trust our electronic gadgets, either.

That voice coming through your Walkman may not really be your late Uncle Charlie.

February 1992

It's All Greek to Me!

If you own a really good dictionary (not an el-cheapo drugstore paperback), look in the front pages and you will find a fascinating surprise. There should be several pages of alphabets and samples of writing from many different foreign languages. Back in the days when I was chasing around the country interviewing witnesses to Fortean events I carried such a dictionary and used it frequently, asking people to pick out the symbols closest to what they had reportedly observed on strange objects and such. Since few percipients are acquainted with foreign languages, they often enthusiastically described what they thought were "hieroglyphics" or "Oriental writing," then, invariably, after studying the dictionary alphabets, they would settle upon Greek letters as what they actually saw.

Almost no one, aside from accomplished linguists, is able to correctly tell the difference between Chinese, Japanese, Korean, and other Oriental languages. There are, of course, many differences, just as true Egyptian hieroglyphics (which are largely pictographs of animals, people and easily identified objects) are very different from Arabic.

For some odd reason, Greek symbols have always played an important role in occult apparitions. Religious tradition tells us that Christianity really began in A.D. 312 when the Emperor Constantine saw a vision of the Greek letters CHI and RO in the sky, then later had a dream in which Christ appeared with those same symbols. Greek letters and words such as "Xeno" (stranger) have had an enigmatic purpose in modern UFO reports. In some of the cases I investigated, the Greek symbols seemed to serve as "triggers" causing the percipients to lapse into a hypnotic trance.

While thus entranced, they experienced hallucinatory episodes that seemed as convincing as reality itself and became the basis for much of the UFO lore.

Phantom Alphabets

A man named Alfred Vail created a new alphabet in the 1840s which quite literally changed the world. (Can you guess what it was? The answer appears later in this column.)

Around the same time, Edgar Allan Poe published his short story, "The Gold Bug," which contained the English alphabet arranged in order of usage. This was extremely valuable in breaking codes. You just have to count the most frequently used symbols or letters in a coded message and it is probably E, the most used letter in the English alphabet.

Making up codes and alphabets is an ancient pursuit. In religion and occultism, whole new languages are frequently introduced. Alchemists, witches, and practitioners of magick have invented thousands of codes to hide their secrets. Even Thomas Jefferson once invented a code machine.

In 1827, a young farm boy named Joseph Smith discovered a set of metal plates buried in New York State. They contained strange carvings which he purportedly translated into the Book of Mormon. It serves as the bible for the Church of Jesus Christ of Latter Day Saints.

The plates were eventually lost but people who claimed to have seen them tried to duplicate some of the symbols and they resembled a number of other occult alphabets, including the "Martian alphabet" later produced by a channeler named Helene in the 1890s.

She would go into trances and speak in voices of other entities. She also visited Mars, presumably with some form of astral projection, describing the buildings there and the small grey beings who inhabited them. A psychologist named Theodore Flournoy wrote a book about Helene and her experiences, titled *From India to the Planet Mars* (1898).

A decade before Helene began her space travels, a New York dentist, John Ballou Newbrough, underwent a series of mystical experiences which led to the creation of *Oahspe*, a nine-hundred-page book that appeared to be another new bible. Newbrough wrote it on the brand-new invention called the typewriter. He didn't know how to type, but he got up very early every morning and hammered away at it for an hour or two. He also produced numerous drawings and designs through automatic writing. Naturally, this included a detailed alphabet for a language called Panic. (Pan was *Oahspe*'s name for the very first inhabited land on earth.) Many of the symbols in Panic bear an interesting resemblance to those of the Mormon plates and the 1898 Martian alphabet.

Panic was more complicated than most occult languages because it dealt with sounds. That is, every true written language must be based on sounds, while codes are based on existing alphabets. To oversimplify this as an example, early Oriental languages described things by the sound they made. The spoken word for "dog" would thus be a barking sound and the written word would have to somehow suggest that sound. To carry this a step further, the spoken word would be dependent on the actual physical structure of the mouth and larynx of the speaker. This is slightly different in different races, so their spoken and written languages are different.

Helene's delusionary Martians might have been lipless and/or tongueless, so their language would be radically different from ours and the symbols of their alphabet would reflect this. In fact, they might not resemble anything we could recognize as a language. Unfortunately, it was clear that Helene's Martian alphabet was primarily a code of symbols substituted for our alphabet. Therefore, it was very likely a product of her unconscious mind. On the other hand, Panic could have been a real language in itself.

Now that you are thoroughly bewildered, let's return to Alfred Vail. In the 1840s, Mr. Vail was employed as the assistant to a famous painter named Samuel F. B. Morse. While Morse tinkered with batteries and switches, perfecting his telegraph, Vail figured out an alphabet that could be reduced to electrical signals—dots and dashes. For example, the much-used letter E became a single dot and T, another much-used letter, became a dash. Seldom-used letters were composed of more involved dots and dashes. In a very real sense, Vail invented a whole new language. As often happens in business, his boss took the credit and it became the "Morse Code." Alfred Vail became lost in the shuffle of history. But everyone who has ever learned it and used it realizes that it is a language of sounds, just as the jungle drums of Africa are—or were—a language instead of a simple code.

For a century, the Morse Code was a major tool in communication, used by railroads, ships, aircraft, newspapers, and industry generally. Millions of people earned their living as telegraphers, and everyone who punched a telegraph key had his or her own distinctive, easily recognized style.

Gradually, however, the use of teletypes and other devices have superseded the telegraph, but ham radio operators still have to learn and use the Morse Code.

Languages of the Gods

Richard Shaver, the founder of modern ufology, heard voices in his head in the 1940s. They taught him a new language which he called "Mantong," yet another variation on Panic. Soon all kinds of alien languages were being introduced into the UFO field, and there were Martian and Venusian alphabets galore. The books and contactee pamphlets of the 1950s are filled with many examples, all of them crudely based on our alphabet rather than upon sounds. Some were received over radios and television sets but most appeared via automatic writing or through channeling.

In recent years, NASA scientists have gotten into the act by devising mathematical forms of communication for SETI, broadcasting dots and dashes into outer space in the hopes that somebody out there might pick them up and figure out how to assemble them into symbols and pictographs.

With the advent of computers, other new languages such as ASCII have been developed so we can talk to our machines and they can communicate with us. (This article is being written in ASCII.) We have even learned the basics of the sounds used by whales, dolphins, and elephants to communicate with each other.

But we still have trouble talking to UFOs because too few ufophiles speak ancient Greek.

March 1992

Black Rain

We've done it again!

Ever since the Persian Gulf war, black rain has been coming down over northern India and the Himalayas. It is caused, of course, by the oil wells that have been burning in Kuwait and sending up volumes of black smoke. Needless to say, black, oil-laden rainwater is not drinkable. We still don't know what long-range effect this will have on the people, animals, and plants of that distant region but you can be sure it won't be a positive one.

In 1991, our shuttle astronauts orbiting the Earth reported that a large part of the planet was shrouded in dirty clouds of pollution. Some of these clouds were probably hovering over the place where you live. Earlier movie footage taken by astronauts shows the spread of ugly brown and black patches at the mouths of rivers and around lakes on our little globe. We're fouling up our world so fast that the pace can hardly be measured.

At a recent lecture, someone asked me to describe the human race and its meaning. I said that we were like fleas on a dog and that we were rapidly multiplying and consuming our host. While some of us labor to find a spiritual meaning for our existence and some great cosmic significance to our being, the bitter facts of the modern world are that we have lost control of our civilization, that we are willfully destroying all of the ecological systems that have nourished us for thousands of years, and that we are not only running out of food in many areas, but we are also facing severe water shortages because we have ruined the watersheds.

According to the best available U.N. studies, one-third of the population of Africa has AIDS. The natives of the once-idyllic islands of the Pacific now spend their days drinking beer and smoking cigarettes while waiting for their welfare checks. Mount Everest is littered with garbage from the scores of expeditions that assault the peak every year.

If someone from another planet was ever dumb enough to pay us a visit, they would undoubtedly hold their nose(s) and take off immediately for more placid areas of the galaxy.

Red Snow and Green Skies

Back in the late 1940s, there was one strange summer when the skies in the Northeast were green for months. The official explanation was that this was caused by tremendous forest fires somewhere in northern Canada. We all accepted this blandly. There have been many forest fires since but the sky has never turned that green again.

Nearly every winter, red snow falls somewhere in Europe. The newspapers always note this without enthusiasm, usually adding that the snow was red because it contained red sand from the Sahara desert! This has become the widely accepted explanation for the phenomenon. Part of my youth was misspent on the Sahara Desert and I never saw any red sand there. It is possible, of course, that there may be a patch of red somewhere, maybe in Sid Ifni, but it would take a whale of a windstorm to carry it from Africa to England where many of the red snows occur. Also, sand is quite heavy and is not likely to remain suspended in the upper atmosphere for very long.

Sand is common silica. If you heat it, it melts and cools to form glass. It is possible that our red snow contains some form of red silicon and the college professors who have examined it cursorily have decided it was just sand. Red silicon may belong in that same mysterious category as the purplish liquid that is found frequently at UFO sites. It is plain old silicon, too, and dries to a cellophane-like substance. The red silicon could have been in a liquid state at one point and became enmeshed in the storm clouds that produced snow. Unfortunately, if we accept this we have to be able to explain where the red silicon came from. We can't explain the purple globs so we aren't likely to be able to explain red globs in the sky, either.

Stars at Noon

There are not only blobs of glop on the ground and in the clouds, there also seem to be truly gigantic opaque objects drifting through space. From time to time, one of these monstrous things floats into our solar system and crosses between the sun and the Earth. When this happens, we suddenly find ourselves in almost complete darkness, sometimes for many months.

Ancient records contain many references to these periods of sudden darkness. They are mentioned in the Bible. Roman histories cite several. In the year A.D. 536 "the sun suffered an eclipse which lasted a whole year and two months, so that very little of his light was seen; men said that something had clung to the sun from which it would never be able to disentangle itself," according to Gregorius Abu'l-Faragius.

In many instances, the sky went black during the day and was so dark that the stars became clearly visible. This indicates that the blackness was not caused by something in the atmosphere but by something coming between the Earth and the Sun…just as the Moon blots out the Sun in a normal eclipse.

But what could be that gigantic? It would have to be bigger than the Sun itself. If it were some celestial body, it would also exert tremendous gravity and it would disrupt the motion of the planets as it soared through. Could it be a cloud of cosmic dust or a mass of red silicon?

In A.D. 1547 both the elder and younger Gemma recorded "the sun appeared for three days as if it were suffused by blood, while at the same time many stars were visible at noon." Aha! A bloody Sun! Was a red blob crossing in front of it?

Polluted Space

More than seven thousand pieces of junk now orbit the Earth. Some of them are pieces of old rockets. There is also a glove, an expensive camera, and all sorts of things that were jettisoned by the astronauts and the cosmonauts in the past thirty years. Our upper atmosphere is almost as polluted as the Atlantic Ocean. NASA issues a regular catalog of what's up there.

Could it be that our entire solar system is also polluted?

Are there red and purple blobs drifting around up there, occasionally even blotting out the Sun?

Twice during the 1960s I saw great blobs drifting in our own atmosphere. There are big lumps of blackness up there that are salient parts of the UFO mystery. People all over the world have seen them and, typically, no one has bothered to investigate them.

One night outside of Ravenswood, West Virginia, in 1967, I saw a gigantic, formless black mass cross the night sky, blotting out the stars and the clouds. It had no lights and made no noise.

Again, a few months after that, near Cherry Hill, New Jersey, I saw another one of these mysterious amoeba-like things soar quickly across the night sky.

Whatever they are, these objects are in the Earth's atmosphere. It is unlikely that they are spaceships just as it is very unlikely that the things that blot out the Sun are machines. Space is so vast and we are so tiny we will probably never know what is really out there any more than a humble flea really knows the true shape and nature of the animal it is riding. All we really know is that there are layers upon layers of pollution in our world and in our universe and it can only get worse.

April 1992

Mysteries of the North

Until the 1950s the North and South Poles were considered almost totally inaccessible and very mysterious. Only a few hardy explorers had dared to approach them, and several died terrible deaths in those frozen wastelands. A rich folklore sprang up around the poles where, as we all know, only Santa Claus and his elves are able to live. A weird subculture was even devoted to the notion that dinosaurs and a lost race of ancient beings still thrived at the North Pole, or inside a great hole there. Volumes have been written claiming that flying saucers are based in that hole.

Many of the mysteries that once swirled about the poles have now been dispelled. We are rapidly building scientific cities in Antarctica and planeloads of tourists flock there every summer. A number of airlines cross directly over the North Pole daily, often circling so their passengers can claim to have been there. All kinds of expeditions have now traversed the poles, and submarines have even sailed under the North Pole. A couple of years ago, an adventurous woman even tried to travel there alone by dogsled but had to abandon the effort when the ice floes began to break up under her feet.

Strange Clouds of Dust

In the 1800s there were several instances in which ships venturing above the Arctic Circle ran into enigmatic clouds of dust. According to Charles Fort and other purveyors of the peculiar such as author Jack Scaparro, disgruntled sailors in the bleak, frozen north sometimes found themselves sweeping the dust off the decks of their ships.

Nobel Prize winner Dr. Fridtjof Nansen noted in his book *Farthest North* that one of his expeditions to the North Pole had to turn back because of the severe dust storms. "What is the use of going on?" he wrote in his log. "Nothing but dust, dust, dust!"

Dust in the middle of an ocean where there is nothing but snow and ice for thousands of miles?

Our old reliable "experts" explained that all that dust came from volcanoes. What volcanoes? The experts never said.

Nansen was puzzled, too, by driftwood floating in the high latitudes.

Another famed explorer, Lt. Commander Adolphus W. Greely, also commented on the driftwood in the Arctic. The nearest source of wood had to be many hundreds of miles to the south. He also reported seeing birds of unknown species, and even butterflies. Butterflies! He wrote that the mysteries of the Arctic were so numerous that he found it necessary to alter his original notes and understate them, lest he be open to charges of gross exaggeration.

Foxes, hares, and even spiders and mosquitoes were found by Arctic expeditions, along with pollen and my personal favorite, red snow. "The strange stories and records of Polar explorers can go on indefinitely. They only seem to deepen the mystery," Scaparro observed in *Lost Continents Beyond the Poles*. "The advent of the space program has failed to offer enlightenment."

Andrée's Balloon Vanishes

On July 11, 1897, three men soared into history in a large balloon headed for the North Pole. Their disappearance triggered one of the oddest series of sightings in modern UFO history.

The head of the expedition was the seasoned Arctic explorer S. A. Andrée. He was accompanied by Nils Strindberg and Knut Fraenkel, two rugged young scientists. Their balloon, the *Eagle*, was "state of the art" for 1897. It was huge, sturdy, and well equipped, carrying enough provisions to see the men through many weeks if necessary. There was no radio in those days, but they carried several trained carrier pigeons and also planned to toss message-laden bottles into the water at intervals—a primitive but time-proven means of communication.

As the *Eagle* rose from the tip of Spitsbergen, the whole world held its collective breath. Everyone was enthralled with Arctic exploration, and Andrée's plans were creating headlines in every country. As the days stretched into weeks, only one carrier pigeon turned up. It landed, exhausted, on the Norwegian ship *Alken* on July 15, about one hundred miles northeast of the *Eagle's* starting point. The message it bore was from Andrée and stated that all was well on July 13. The balloon was moving slowly northwards on schedule.

No more pigeons were found. It soon became obvious that the *Eagle* was lost.

The newspapers began to worry and speculate on Andrée's fate. Then a very curious thing began to happen.

People all over the world, particularly in the northern latitudes, started to see balloons in the sky. Most thought they were seeing Andrée's missing balloon.

The Great Balloon Epidemic

Balloons—any kind of balloon—were a very rare sight in the 1800s. They were largely confined to county fairs and seldom traveled more than a few miles. Nevertheless, Andrée and his comrades seemed to be everywhere at once.

A memorial volume published in 1906 by the Swedish Society for Anthropology cataloged many of the sightings. Author Vilhjalmur Stefansson detailed several of them in his classic *Unsolved Mysteries of the Arctic* (1938).

A number of ships reported seeing balloons in the sky or wrecked in the water, even though none of them were anywhere near the route of the Andrée expedition. For example, the crew of the *Saimia* off the coast of

Greenland said that they saw a balloon traveling at an altitude of about one thousand feet and moving in a northerly direction.

The newspaper *Nya Vexiobladet* reported that "an elderly woman of this town, whose truthfulness is beyond question, says that on the evening of July 17 she was about to go to bed, and had gone to her window to pull down the blind, when through a window she noticed something which looked exactly like a balloon with drag ropes and a net. It had a gondola with apparently a man standing in it."

A few months earlier, most of the United States had been gripped by sightings of "airships" and mischievous newspapermen embellished the stories until it became almost impossible for later researchers to separate the facts from the fiction. In contrast, the Andrée balloon stories appeared in isolated, unsophisticated newspapers throughout the Arctic Circle.

One of the most interesting series of balloon sightings took place in a very remote section of Siberia around the Tunguska River where, a decade later, the celebrated "meteor" would crash and explode, destroying a vast area of forest.

Stefansson noted: "There proved to be two chief world centers for the balloon reports. In Asia it was the Yenisei valley; in North America it was British Columbia."

An Unhappy Ending

On July 9, 1930, a ship stopped at bleak, uninhabited White Island, northeast of Spitsbergen, and discovered what was left of Andrée and his party. Their balloon had crashed on July 14, 1897, one day after they had sent the pigeon. The three men had worked their way over the ice floes to the island. They had food and ammunition but their only shelter was a flimsy tent made from the balloon cloth. They probably froze to death.

The mystery was solved. Or was it? If their balloon went down three days after take-off, what were those things people all over the far north continued to see in the sky for many months afterwards? The "airships" of North

America were everywhere that year. Andrée's disappearance just gave the newspapers and the witnesses a frame of reference for the strange phenomena.

May 1992

The Truth About Crashes

If a single-engine Cessna airplane should run out of gas and come crashing down in your backyard you would soon be hosting carloads of police, sheriffs, FAA inspectors, and hordes of curious citizens. They would be swarming all over your property, taking pictures, making measurements, and carefully sifting dirt. All of these would be normal procedures for an aviation accident.

However, if you should hear weird sounds in that same backyard one night and should see a glowing object sitting in that same dirt, burning the ground and initiating a Spielberg movie fantasy, guess who would answer your frantic phone call?

If you're lucky, a deputy sheriff might turn up three or four days later, make a cursory inspection of the burned grass, and depart with a whimsical smile. If you called the nearest U.S. Air Force base, a polite young lieutenant might drive around to see you a month or two after the event. (More likely, nobody would ever come by.)

This non-scenario has been repeated thousands of times in the past forty years. Only in a few well-known incidents have the authorities demonstrated any interest in the unknown crashing objects that keep pelting our landscape.

For example, when traces of something odd appeared in a woods near Glassboro, New Jersey, in 1964, the Secretary of the Air Force himself, one Harold Brown, paid a visit. But the famous crashed aerial object at Flatwoods, West Virginia, in 1952, failed to excite any official interest at all even though there were several witnesses, physical evidence, and a strange gas that caused the death of a dog.

One wonders why they have had the change in attitude.

Holes in the Ice

You may remember what happened in Wakefield, New Hampshire, back in January 1977. It received national publicity in all the major newspapers and newsmagazines. A building contractor named William McCarthy discovered a hole in the ice covering a pond on his farm during a heavy snowstorm. The ice was about fifteen inches thick, but something had punched a hole in it and penetrated the frozen bottom of the pond.

Mr. McCarthy was convinced there was something unusual in his pond. The Air Force wasn't interested, but a team from the local Highway Department finally appeared and poked around the hole. As word spread, a civil defense crew also arrived with Geiger counters to see if the hole was radioactive. Soon helicopters bearing television people were landing in the snow and the whole country waited breathlessly for some object from outer space to be dug up.

Meldrim Thompson, Jr., governor of New Hampshire, got into the act when he held a press conference and declared: "There is no object on the bottom of the pond. I am glad the whole thing is false because this could have been detrimental to the citizens of New Hampshire."

As often happens in these cases, the McCarthy family was hounded by a parade of unwelcome visitors, reporters, and UFO buffs. Mrs. Dorothy McCarthy was quoted in the press as making the old, familiar lament, "If a hole appears ever again, we're not going to say anything."

So we have a double-barreled problem here. In most cases nobody pays any attention at all to these events, causing the witnesses to get riled over the neglect. But when the news media does pick up on these things and the witnesses find themselves the focus of unwelcome publicity, they get even more riled! It is always a no-win situation.

Space Droppings

Each year strange, glowing objects come hurtling out of the sky, crashing into lakes, ponds, and reservoirs all over the world. As usual, nobody has made a systematic study of these things. Would natural objects such as meteors single out bodies of water? Not very likely. What attracts these things to water and, more importantly, what happens to them after they go beneath the surface?

In 1965 and 1966, the Wanaque Reservoir in New Jersey was the site of many bizarre UFO incidents. These luminous whatzits struck the water on several occasions. Searches of the reservoir were held in vain. I joined the late Ivan Sanderson on searches of other bodies of water in New Jersey during that period and nothing was ever found.

Later, when I lived in the Catskill Mountains two hours north of New York City, I found that some of the remote mountain lakes were frequently assaulted by falling, glowing globs. One family living close to one of these lakes kept a log of their sightings—which were numerous and enigmatic.

Add to these the many, many reports of "airplanes," sometimes "burning airplanes," which crash into harbors and bays all over the world, inciting extensive but futile searches. Often there are so many witnesses, and they are all so certain that they saw a real crash, that the searches go on for days without locating a single piece of debris or even an oil slick. It is quite possible, even very probable, that most of these "crashes" are really more globs of unidentified cosmic glop.

Norway and Sweden have many lakes which are visited annually by falling aerial objects. Again, there have been extensive searches of some of the bodies of water with the usual results.

When I was visiting Sweden in 1976, a hiker had discovered a mysterious hole in the ground deep in a patch of forest. Scientists from the Swedish government took an interest in this hole and built a road to it so they could do some serious digging. People in the area had reported seeing something fall from the sky into the woods.

A Keystone comedy quickly developed. Government divers and scientists labored over the water-filled hole by day. When they left at 5:00 p.m. teams of local UFO buffs would arrive and probe during the night. They were all quite convinced that there was something in the mud at the bottom of this murky pit.

Readers of this column are aware that I am the world's leading authority on holes in the ground—a holeologist if you will. There doesn't seem to be much demand for this profession, but somebody has got to do it. In any case, I dutifully made the long trip to the Swedish forest with a group of UFO-philes and soberly peered into the hole, making knowing comments such as, "'This is the most mysterious hole I have ever seen."

They never did find anything there. Like the hole in New Hampshire it simply appeared, didn't make any sense, but got a lot of people excited.

The Whole Hole Business

How can we possibly investigate these space droppings? First, someone must screen the Fortean literature and catalog all these events. They seem to follow the well-established patterns of other Fortean events clustering around the solstices and following specific cycles.

The next logical step would be to stake out one of the lakes where these things are most recurrent and, using radar and other instruments, ascertain their physicality, velocity, and general characteristics. They don't seem to generate heat, even when striking ice or cold water, so their luminosity may not be caused by molecular change.

That is, they are not like a lump of glowing coal. They may be emitting a form of cold light.

It is, of course, very difficult to interest any government-sponsored scientists in examining this mystery and few, if any, big corporations are likely to spend money on such a profitless investigation. So we are left, as usual, with a gang of amateur holeologists stumbling around in the woods in the dark, very unsure of what exactly they would do if they actually found something at the bottom of one of these holes.

June 1992

Wild Talents

In each generation there are millions of people who inherit or somehow come to possess wild talents that make them different from the rest of the human race. Perhaps you are one of them and that is why you are reading this book. It makes you feel less alone to know there are others out there whose view of reality is slightly askew. They (we) see, hear, and feel things that more normal mortals cannot perceive.

During the Vietnamese war, the U.S. military discovered that about fifteen percent of our soldiers had the ability to dowse and that they could locate enemy tunnels using forked sticks. Dowsing, a time-honored wild talent, became one of our military secrets.

Astral projection, another ancient wild talent, was also the subject of experiments by the CIA and the Defense Department. There had been rumors and unconfirmed gossip in World War I that the Germans had used astral projectionists successfully as spies. People who had out-of-body experiences (OBEs) seemed very promising as strategic sneaks capable of penetrating the most closely guarded defenses of any enemy.

Millions of people apparently have this ability. The recent studies of near-death experiences (NDEs), which seem to have some relationship to the OBEs, are giving us deeper insights into the phenomenon. It could be that a very large number of us have latent out-of-body talents.

From the earliest surveys and studies of the British Society for Psychical Research in the last century there has been a clear indication that about fifteen percent of any population is involved in supernatural experiences of some sort, while the other eighty-five percent scoffs and sneers and joins skeptical organizations.

In my own tenuous efforts, such as polling audiences in TV studios and at lectures, I have found that from twelve to fifteen percent always claim to have seen UFOs, ghosts, or angels; experienced prophetic dreams or ESP; or otherwise shared in whatever my particular topic was. Cynics might point out that this is proof that about fifteen percent are merely candidates for the funny farm.

The Looney Poll

Over the years, various psychiatric associations have, in fact, attempted to make learned estimates of the segment of the population that really is "around the bend." In 1980, one group of head shrinkers endeared themselves to New Yorkers by claiming that at least eighty percent of everyone who lives in mighty Manhattan is completely bonkers! Other studies insist that over two million full-fledged lunatics are walking around loose in this country at any given time. Old World War II army studies placed the hopelessly crackpotted population at around four percent.

In other words, four people out of every one hundred do not have both oars in the water. These four are supposed to be our much-maligned "lunatic fringe."

Can these people successfully dowse for water? Can they see with crystal clarity future events that later come true?

Years ago, during my army days, I knew a young soldier who seemed quite sane except for one peculiarity. He could point his finger at a lock and it would snap open without him touching it!

He could do this with any kind of lock, from a simple padlock to a complex tumbler lock. No trickery seemed to be involved. It was his wild talent. I don't know what happened to him. Perhaps he went on to become the world's greatest safecracker.

There was once a newsletter devoted to people who could cause street lights to blow out just by looking at them. We have all had that experience at some time or other but there are those who have the rare (and useless) ability to extinguish street lamps whenever they feel like it.

Like the fictitious Dr. Doolittle, there are some who can actually communicate with animals. Weirdest of all, there really are people who can perform magic—distort reality itself—with the power of their minds. In other ages they were called wizards, warlocks, and witches, and were often greatly feared. They did not study books of forbidden knowledge and ancient lore. They did not burn candles and utter incomprehensible incantations. They were born with their powers. As they grow older they become frightened and paranoid. They don't know how to deal with their wild talents. Stage magicians imitate them.

Thousands of people, some of whom are genuine members of the aforementioned four percent, delude themselves into thinking that they, too, can distort reality. They become cult members and engage in a multitude of fringe subjects. For example, a man named Ted Owens convinced himself that he could control the outcome of football games and that he derived his powers from flying saucers. Did he get rich betting on sports? No. The space people kept letting him down—or so he claimed.

Millions of us are graced with eyes that can see slightly beyond the visible spectrum. There are forms of energy all around us that normally cannot be seen but these special people are able to catch glimpses, usually in their peripheral vision, of shadowy forms and shapes that come and go with suddenness. This wild talent has spawned all kinds of religious, supernatural, and pseudoscientific beliefs. These visions may be real enough to the percipient but they are not quite part of our reality. They are a part of another reality that interacts with ours and sometimes even intersects completely with our very narrow space-time continuum. Eighty-five percent of our population cannot even sense this interaction and very few of the gifted fifteen percent are interested in trying to communicate their perceptions to them.

Who needs to get into such pointless hassles? Assorted cults, frames of reference, and belief systems do spring up, however, based upon the fragmented testimony of the fifteen-percenters. In many cases, a vast cult literature even develops and absurdities become reality to people who have never experienced anything, have never seen anything, and never will. The cult literature feeds upon itself, multiplying like a fungus.

Dragons are born out of the shadows along with all kinds of monsters, spaceships, demons, and demigods. Our libraries are filled with such works. The readers of this material do welcome hassles and controversies and love to fight with each other.

The actual witnesses—our fifteen-percenters—cringe into the background.

Hypnotic Spells

Some people are natural hypnotists, real living Svengalis. They can hand a railroad conductor a blank piece of paper and he will punch it, thinking it is a real ticket.

If you read any thorough history of hypnotism you will learn about all the cults that sprang up around persuasive mind-manipulators. Literally thousands of weird beliefs were born from the machinations of unconscious minds unleashed by hypnosis. Remember Bridey Murphy in the 1950s? Sometimes the use of drugs is combined with hypnotic techniques, producing even more bizarre results.

Our fifteen-percenters don't need drugs or hypnosis (although certain meditative practices can induce self-hypnosis) to release their wild talents. They will continue to baffle and enrage the skeptics and the untalented eighty-five percent as they wend their way along that narrow tightwire that separates our reality from the Twilight Zone.

Afterword

For more than ten years, John Keel's column in FATE magazine delighted and challenged readers. Whether he was revealing the details of the Mothman investigation, infuriating supporters of the Roswell crashed-spaceship theory, or amusing us with tales of human stupidity, Keel was one of FATE's most essential contributors. Watch for future volumes of *The Best of John Keel*, sure to confound, amaze, and take you Beyond the Known!

—ANDREW HONIGMAN

To order additional copies of this book,
please send full amount plus $5.00 for
postage and handling for the first book and
$1.00 for each additional book.

Send orders to:

Galde Press, Inc.
PO Box 460
Lakeville, Minnesota 55044-0460

Credit card orders call 1–800–777–3454
Phone (952) 891–5991 • Fax (952) 891–6091
Visit our website at http://www.galdepress.com

Write for our free catalog.